KICKING OVER SACRED COWS

Charles Capps

Unless otherwise indicated, all
Scripture quotations are taken from the
King James Version of the Bible

KICKING OVER SACRED COWS
  10th Printing

Kicking Over Sacred Cows
ISBN-10: 0-9747513-1-6
ISBN-13: 978-0-9747513-1-3
Formerly ISBN 0-89274-409-X
Copyright © 1983, 1987 by Charles Capps
P.O. Box 69
England, Arkansas 72046

Published by Capps Publishing
P.O. Box 69
England, Arkansas 72046

Table of Contents

Chapter 1

THE CHASTENING OF
THE LORD

First, I will share with you some keys of rightly dividing the Word of Truth. Then we're going to kick over some sacred cows. Many of the people in India worship cows, but would not dare eat them. The very thing God provided for food holds them in bondage. The blessing becomes a curse when they refuse to partake of it.

There are some sacred cow scriptures in the Bible that are holding many people in bondage. The Word of God was given to fulfill the needs in our life. But when people worship the scripture and wouldn't dare partake of the Bread of Life, then it holds them in bondage. These are certain preconceived ideas that become a curse because people don't rightly divide the Word of God.

Knowledge Of The Truth.

We have all heard people talk about the chastening of

1

the Lord. Well, what did the Bible say about it? All some people know about the Bible is what they heard that somebody said they thought they heard somebody say about it.

Well, that's not good enough. Let's find out what the Bible really said about chastening. **Then apply that to your situation in life by rightly dividing God's Word. When you do that, the knowledge of the truth will set you free.**

God said through His prophet Hosea, *My people are destroyed for lack of knowledge.* (Hosea 4:6) You see, he didn't say God's people were destroyed because the devil was so great or powerful. But he said, *My people are destroyed for* **lack of knowledge.**

> *31 Then said Jesus to those Jews which believed on him, If ye continue in my word, then are ye my disciples indeed;*
>
> *32 And ye shall know the truth, and the truth shall make you free.* (John 8:31-32)

Notice, it's not **just** the truth that sets you free. Everyone who has the Bible has the truth. But you must have **the knowledge of the truth.** You can't believe any further that you have knowledge. You have to **know the truth** before it can set you free.

When you rightly divide the Word of God, you will kick over some sacred cows.

Faith Pleases God.

But without faith it is impossible to please him, for he that cometh to God must believe that he is and that he is the rewarder of them that diligently seek him. (Hebrews 11:6)

The Word says you can't please God without faith. It's an impossibility. That's because God is a faith God, and all that God has given us, He has given through the avenue of faith. Every promise of God's Word is tapped into through faith. The apostle Paul put it this way: by faith you have access into the grace of God. There is no other way to get into the grace of God only through faith.

Law Of Faith.

Faith is a law. Under the old covenant there was what we call the old law. People had a limited righteousness under the old law. It was through the law of works.

But now our righteousness is through the law of faith. **Faith is the law of the new covenant.** The apostle Paul says in Romans three,

Do we make void the law through faith?

God forbid: yea, we establish the law. (Romans 3:31)

The law he is referring to is the law of the new covenant, which is the law of faith.

Here the Word says, without faith it's impossible to please God, *and he that cometh to God must believe that he is, and that he is a rewarder of them that diligently seek him.* (Heb. 11:6) It's not enough to believe that God exists. We must believe that God is the rewarder of them that diligently seek Him.

God Is Not A Troublemaker.

To please God, first we must come to Him. Then we

3

must believe that He is, and that **He is the rewarder.** He is not the One Who takes away. He is not the One Who causes us problems in life. God is not the troublemaker.

There has been an undercurrent in religious circles which says the trials, the tests, the problems you have in life are designed of God to make you stronger. Then someone said, God led the children of Israel through the wilderness for forty years to perfect them.

Disobedience Brought A Curse.

You ought to check up on the wilderness experience. It wasn't God's will for the children of Israel to spend forty years in the wilderness. Their disobedience caused them to stay there forty years.

Then some suggest that it is the trials and the tests of life that makes our faith stronger. Well, ask yourself: did it make the children of Israel stronger?

No, it didn't make their faith stronger. **It killed them. It will kill you, if you stay there long enough.**

We need to understand that God is a rewarder of them that diligently seek Him.

No Mixture Of Faith.

The children of Israel spent forty years in the wilderness because of disobedience. The Bible says they wouldn't mix any faith with the Word of God. God said, "I have given you the land. It belongs to you. Go in and possess it." But they wouldn't mix any faith with God's Words.

For unto us was the gospel preached, as well as unto them: but the word preached did not profit them, not being mixed with faith in them that heard it. (Hebrews 4:2)

There must be a mixing of our faith with God's Word. We must **believe that He is the rewarder** of them that diligently seek Him. God is a good God.

God is on our side. But millions of people don't know God is on their side. Through religious tradition and preconceived ideas, many have decided that God is a big old gray-headed man with a long beard and a big stick. And if you ever miss it, He's going to slap you down and put His foot on you.

But that is not our heavenly Father. He is the rewarder of them that diligently seek Him.

Jesus: Author Of Faith.

Now let's go to the twelfth chapter of Hebrews.

1 Wherefore seeing we also are compassed about with so great a cloud of witnesses, let us lay aside every weight, and the sin which doth so easily beset us, and let us run with patience the race that is set before us,

2 Looking unto Jesus the author and finisher of our faith... (Hebrews 12:1-2)

This tells you that Jesus is the author of your faith. Jesus is also the finisher of your faith. Notice, it didn't say that trials and tests were the author of your faith. So the question is settled. Jesus is the author.

And who was Jesus? Jesus was **the Word.**

1 In the beginning was the Word, and the Word was with God, and the Word was God.

5

3 All things were made by him; and without him was not any thing made that was made.

14 The word was made flesh and dwelt among us. (And we beheld his glory. . . . (John 1:1,3,14)

Jesus was the Word of God personified. Hebrews twelve actually tells us that the Word is the author of our faith.

Faith's Beginning.

You can better understand that as you go to Romans, the tenth chapter and read what Paul said.

So then faith cometh by hearing, and hearing by the Word of God. (Romans 10:17)

That's where faith begins. Faith has its beginning by hearing the Word of God. But if you don't hear the Word of God, faith won't come. That's why the apostle Paul says,

God hath dealt to every man the measure of faith. (Romans 12:3)

Not **a** measure; **the** measure.

Measuring Faith.

Think about it for a minute. How would you measure faith?

God's Word is filled with faith, and faith comes by hearing the Word of God. Then the only way you could measure faith is to **measure the amount of Word that is in you.**

If someone says, "Well, I just don't have faith to believe God for finances," that means there is a lack of the Word in them concerning the promise of finances.

6

You could be highly developed in your faith concerning healing, if you had been taught healing is for you today. But maybe you had grown up in a church where they were thumbs-down on the prosperity message. If you were taught every Sunday that it is wrong to be prosperous, and to be poor is humility, then more than likely, you will believe you should be poor. Not because it's God's will, but because that's what you believe God's will is, and you want to please God.

The Word of God is the beginning of faith for the promises. That's why an individual could be highly developed in one area, such as healing, and not have any faith in another promise, such as finances, or the baptism of the Holy Spirit.

The Death Of Faith.

We must take God's Word for it. But when we get off God's Word and go toward religious traditional ideas, we make the Word of God of none effect. (Matthew 15:6) So if we take tradition for it instead of what God said about it, then we would have no faith at all in promises that are for us today.

Maybe one person would have great faith in finances, but have no faith at all for healing. They may have been raised in church which taught that healing went out with the apostles. You can understand why someone who had been taught that way from the age of five would believe that way. Their faith for those promises would be dead.

They must have their minds renewed to the Word of God. Men's traditions will make the promise of no effect.

But faith for the promise cometh by hearing the Word of promise.

God Is A Rewarder.

God is a rewarder of them that diligently seek Him. God is not taking away from you when you diligently seek Him. But that's the idea some people get when they read the book of Job.

After I had taught a seminar in a Bible School, a man studying for the ministry wrote me a letter. He said, "Now, I know what you taught concerning Job, that Job got into fear and opened the door to the devil. But I don't believe it that way. I believe God knew that Job was perfect and strong enough to stand it; that's the reason He took everything that he had."

If what that fellow believed were true, then we really would be in trouble. For the Bible admonishes us, *be ye perfect as God is perfect.* So, according to his theology, if we were to attain that perfection, then we would lose our family and all of our possessions.

But Proverbs says,

The blessing of the Lord, it maketh rich, and he addeth no sorrow with it. (Proverbs 10:22)

Calamity is not a blessing. Poverty is not a blessing. God adds no sorrow to His blessings. Problems don't build your faith. Jesus is the author of your faith. God's Word, not the trials and problems, will put the finishing touches to your faith.

Trials And Troubles Are Not Blessings.

With any trial or test that comes your way, if you will act on the Word of God in it, you will come out of that situation stronger. When that happens, some people will say, "Well, that trial made them stronger. That's why God sent it their way."

But that is simply not true. God didn't send the trial. The devil sent the trial to get the Word out of you. We have only but to read Mark, the fourth chapter to find that this is the work of the devil. Jesus tells you five things that Satan uses to get the Word out of you.

17 . . . when affliction or persecution ariseth **for the word's sake, immediately they are offended.**

19 And the cares of this world, and the deceitfulness of riches, and the lusts of other things entering in, choke the word, and it becometh unfruitful. (Mark 4:17,19)

Those things were not designed to increase your faith, to make you more like Jesus. They were designed to get God's Word out of you. Sometimes people say, "Well, all of these trials and tests of life are the chastening of the Lord."

Then you have heard others say, "Everything that happens to you in life is the will of God for you. That's God's way of chastening you."

If that were true, there would be no need to pray or resist the devil.

But those things which happen to you in life are not necessarily God's will. In Hebrews twelve there is a chastening of the Lord that is for your good. Let's look at what the scriptures really say on this matter.

> *And ye have forgotten the exhortation which speaketh unto you as unto children, My son, despise not thou the chastening of the Lord, nor faint when thou art rebuked of him.* (Hebrews 12:5)

Underline the phrase, *speaketh unto you as unto children.* If you miss this phrase in this passage you will miss the context of this twelfth chapter. Notice it says, *And ye have forgotten the exhortation,* or, the thing that was spoken to you.

> *6 For whom the Lord loveth he chasteneth, and scourgeth every son whom he receiveth.*
>
> *7 If ye endure chastening, God dealeth with you as with sons; for what son is he whom the father chasteneth not?* (Hebrews 12:6-7)

Now that's a fair question. Is there any father here on earth who has a child and wouldn't teach his child? The word "chasten" means to child train. If you don't get a clear understanding of what the word means before you start, then you will miss the whole point. **Chasten means to child train.**

You will understand this when go you back to verse 5: *And ye have forgotten the exhortation which speaketh unto you as unto children.* He is talking about training as you would train a child.

The scripture is not inferring that God is sending some calamity your way to teach you. That would be child abuse, not child training. But yet, some say "God sends sickness to chasten His children."

10

Don't Throw Away Common Sense.

I have heard it preached over national television that sometimes God will make you sick and send troubles to you. That made me appreciate the song that David Ingles sings. "If God was going to give you sickness, He would have to steal it first." God doesn't have any disease. As someone so aptly stated, sickness couldn't come from heaven, because there isn't any sickness in heaven.

It doesn't take long to figure that out, if you just use some common sense. It's a mystery to me why some people, when they get religious, lose all their common sense and quit thinking.

Nurture A Child.

Before we go back to Hebrews twelve, let's look at Ephesians six.

And, ye fathers, provoke not your children to wrath: but bring them up in the nurture and admonition of the Lord. (Ephesians 6:4)

Notice the word "nurture". This is the very same Greek word that is translated "chastening" or "chastisement" in Hebrews twelve. To **nurture** a child is quite different from some of our preconceived ideas of chastening. Most people, when they think about chastening, think God is doing them harm. But chastening is used here in the sense of nurturing.

11

Instruction In Righteousness.

All scripture is given by inspiration of God, and is profitable for doctrine, for reproof, for correction, for instruction in righteousness. (2nd Timothy 3:16)

The same Greek word that is translated "chasten" in Hebrews twelve is translated **instruction** here in this verse. Chastening means to instruct. Strong's Concordance says the meaning is to **train a child.**

Train Or Abuse.

What some people call God's chastisement upon His children is really child abuse. And God does not have anything to do with child abuse.

A friend went to speak at a certain meeting where one of the group gave a testimony of how God gave him cancer to make him humble. My friend got up to teach. He said, "If you don't learn anything else tonight, you're going to learn that God didn't give this fellow cancer."

He said it in love. The man came to him after the service and said, "I appreciate you showing me scripturally. I've never seen that before."

So here's a man who thought God had given him cancer to instruct him. Well, ask yourself this question. If a court of law could prove that you had given your child cancer, what do you think they would do with you?

They'd put you in prison. Wicked men would put you in prison for child abuse. Society will prosecute you for mistreating a child. If you make your child sick, that is child abuse.

12

Doctrines of Devils.

But see how religious tradition has crept in and has driven these wedges into our thinking, until we believe that God is carrying all kinds of calamity and trouble to give out to His children. But it's a lie. My Father is not a child abuser.

Now that's a sacred cow that needs to be kicked over. The devil is perpetrating this lie, and many have fallen for it. The apostle Paul said,

> . . . in the latter times some shall depart from the faith, giving heed to seducing spirits, and doctrines of devils. (1st Timothy 4:1)

If anything comes near to being a doctrine of the devil, it is the idea that God is making you sick, and God is causing you troubles. God and the devil never have changed places, regardless of what anyone says. **God is still a good God, and the devil is still a bad devil.** The devil is not perfecting the church.

Notice Paul says,

> All scripture is given by inspiration of God, and is profitable for doctrine, for reproof, for correction, for instruction in righteousness. (2nd Timothy 3:16)

Instruction is the same word that is translated "chastise." In John's gospel you find these words—*Howbeit when he, the Spirit of truth, is come, he will guide you into all truth.* (John 16:13)

The Holy Spirit, not the devil, will teach you these things. The devil is not perfecting the church.

I heard a certain minister say this; "people blame everything on the devil. But the devil is nothing more than an unwilling servant of God."

I could hardly believe what I was hearing. In other words, he was saying the devil is really working for God. It's hard to see how anyone could think that way, when Jesus Himself said,

The thief cometh not, but for to steal, and to kill, and to destroy. (John 10:10)

The Thief Came To Destroy, Not To Perfect.

John 10:10 is the dividing line of the Bible. *The thief cometh not, but for to steal, and to kill, and to destroy God's creation. He didn't say the devil came to perfect the church, to perfect your faith, to make you more like Jesus.* **Satan came for only three reasons: kill, steal, and destroy.** Then Jesus said, "I am come." Thank God Jesus has come because He has brought us the truth. The law came by Moses, but grace and truth came by Jesus Christ. **Jesus came and told us the truth about the devil.**

If you study only the Old Testament, you will be left in the dark about the devil. For there was very little revealed in the Old Testament about the devil, or how to defeat him.

God didn't reveal much about the devil in the Old Testament because there wasn't much they could do about him. Under the old covenant, they didn't have authority over the devil. The only hope they had was to stay under the covenant. If they got out from under it, they were open game to the devil, and there wasn't much they could do about it. That's why, under the old covenant, the children of Israel suffered at the hands of the destroyer. (1st Corinthians 10:9-10) The King James Bible says the Lord sent serpents among them, and bit them, and much people of Israel died.

It is translated in a causative sense, when it should have been translated in an allowing sense. God told them, "I'm going to allow to come whatever you say in my ear."

Disobedience Brings Destruction.

They said, "We wish we'd have stayed in Egypt. We're going to all die in the wilderness."

Then serpents came among them and bit them, and many died. It is translated that God **sent** the serpents. But ask yourself this question. If they had been obedient to God, would the serpents have come? Would they have died, had they been obedient to God?

The answer is obvious.

Then what caused the serpents to come? **Their disobedience.**

You will find in the Old Testament that they generally believed that everything which happened was from God, for there was very little revealed about the devil. They just assumed that God was behind everything that happened. They believed, if something happened to you, it was God's will. And most of the time, it wasn't God's will at all. By understanding what they believed, we can more readily understand why some of the things were recorded as they were in the Old Testament.

15

Only Sons Are Chastened.

But if ye be without chastisement, whereof all are partakers, then are ye bastards, and not sons. (Hebrews 12:8).

In other words, all of God's children are partakers of chastening. God chastens all of His sons. Then if you are without chastisement, you are illegitimate children, and not sons.

In the light of that verse, if sickness and disease were the chastening of the Lord, **then no sinners would ever be sick.** Notice verse 8; **all the children are partakers of chastening.** But illegitimate children are not. In other words, if you're not a child of God, you wouldn't be chastened of the Lord, because you're not His child. So if sickness and disease and the problems of life were the chastening of the Lord, then no sinners would have any problems nor any sickness. Only Christians would have sickness and problems. But we know that is not true. Everyone faces problems.

Remember, Hebrews twelve is referring to chastening as training a child.

Ask yourself this. If you had a small child and he walked up to a stove with the burner burning, what would you do? You would probably say, "Ah, ah, ah! Don't touch that! It's hot! It will burn you!"

You would train that child with words. You would communicate to that child what will happen if he touches the burner.

Now, if that child touches it while you're not looking, then you didn't burn the child, nor cause it to happen.

The child then brought it on himself by disobedience. You told the child what would happen if he disobeyed.

This is what happened when God told the children of Israel what was going to happen if they did certain things contrary to the law. When they did it, then it was translated that God **sent** the serpents.

Chastening Is Not Abuse.

Suppose, while you are not looking, your child does touch the stove and gets burned, and somebody says, "Look what you did to your child! If you hadn't told him it was hot, it wouldn't have burned him."

This is how God gets the blame for so many calamities, when He didn't have a thing to do with them. It was not the instruction that caused them to be burned, but their disobedience.

Neither would you take the child's hand, stick it on the stove, burn big blisters on its hand, and say, "Now, I did that to teach you not to touch the stove."

If you did that, they would put you in jail for child abuse.

If God lived here on earth and did some of the things that many Christians accuse Him of doing, He'd spend all of His time in the penitentiary for child abuse. But that is not the way our heavenly Father trains and instructs His children.

Fleshly Father Chastens Flesh.

Here is another key.

Furthermore we have had fathers of our flesh which corrected us, and we gave them reverence: shall we not much rather be in subjection unto the Father of spirits, and live? (Hebrews 12:9)

Now notice, he said we are subject to the **fathers of our flesh,** which correct us. **Sometimes, if they correct through the flesh, it produces physical pain.** When you apply the "board of education" to the "seat of learning," there is some pain involved. If we are in subjection to the *fathers of our flesh which corrected us, and we give them reverence,* **shall we not much rather be in subjection unto the Father of spirits, and live?** (v.9)

Father Of Spirits Chastens Spirit.

In other words, the Father of Spirits is our heavenly Father. He is a spirit, and He is going to chasten us by spiritual means. **He chastens our spirits, not our physical bodies.** He deals with us in the spirit. Several scriptures put this to be spiritual chastening. Jesus said the Words I speak to you, they are Spirit—they are life. (John 6:63) In Ephesians five, Paul talked about cleansing the church by the washing of water by the Word. It's the Word of God that chastens us. The reason the unbelievers are not chastened of the Lord is that **they won't receive His Word.**

Chasten By The Word.

God chastens you with the Word. Psalm 94:12 says,

Blessed is the man whom thou chastenest, O Lord, and teachest him out of thy law. (Psalm 94:12)

Blessed is the man God instructs or teaches out of His Word, or is chastened by that Word.

The apostle Paul said to the Corinthian church, "I robbed other churches to do you service." He chastened them with his words. He told them not to muzzle the ox that treadeth the corn.

Chastening Of The Word Makes Partaker Holy.

The reason sinners are not chastened is that they won't receive God's Word. God's Word is there, but unbelievers will not receive it. So there is no chastening to unbelievers, because they won't receive the Word of God. But they sow to the flesh and reap of the flesh corruption—and then many want to blame it on God.

9 . . . be in subjection unto the Father of spirits, and live?

10 For they verily for a few days chastened us after their own pleasure; but he for our profit, that we might be partakers of his holiness. (Hebrews 12:9-10)

Here he says our fathers in the flesh *chasten us after their own pleasure; but **he (God) for our profit.*** In other words, if God does chasten you, it's going to profit you; *that we might be **partakers of his holiness.*** Every chastening is going to make you a partaker of holiness, and it is the Word instructing you in the ways of God.

Then, if sickness and disease were the chastening of the Lord, everyone who was sick would become more holy.

But you know just being sick and in the hospital doesn't make you more holy. The Word of God instructs us in holiness.

19

Chastening Yields Righteousness.

Now no chastening for the present seemeth to be joyous, but grievous: nevertheless afterward it yieldeth the peaceable fruit of righteousness unto them which are exercised thereby. (Hebrews 12:11)

This verse declares that chastening will produce the "fruit of righteousness." Here again, if sickness and disease were the chastening, then the more sickness you suffered, the more righteous you would become. So you can see how ridiculous it would be to say the chastening of the Lord is sickness. That would be taking the scripture completely out of context.

Chastening Cleanses Partaker.

In John fifteen, Jesus said,

Now ye are clean through the word which I have spoken unto you. (John 15:3)

The Word cleanses.

I've heard people say, "Well, you know, it's the problems and calamities that makes people come to the Lord."

But in Romans two, the apostle Paul said,

. . . the goodness of God leadeth thee to repentance. (Romans 2:4)

I remember years ago what my dad said when he gave his heart to the Lord. He said "The thing that brought me in was that God just blessed me so much, even though I wasn't living for Him. . . ."

. . . Despiseth then the riches of his goodness and forbearance and longsuffering; not knowing that the goodness of God leadeth thee to repentance? (Romans 2:4)

This scripture is exactly the opposite to what most people believe. They believe God will just whip you into line, and make you do certain things.

If God were going to do that, then He would make everybody get saved today, and we'd all go in the millennium in the morning. But God doesn't violate man's will.

God's instruction to us is, as it were, child training. He trains us by His sayings. The scripture tells us to not do certain things. For if we do. we open the door to the devil, and trouble will come.

By that instruction, you gain the knowledge of God. When you gain the knowledge of God, you gain faith in God. If you don't know what God has promised, you can't have faith to believe Him for it. Jesus (the Word) is the author and the finisher of our faith. And they that come to God must believe that He is the **rewarder of them that diligently seek Him.**

He is not the punisher of them that seek Him. He is not the tormentor of those that seek him. **He is the rewarder.**

That's our heavenly Father.

Chapter 2

WHAT ABOUT JOB?

Study to shew thyself approved unto God, a workman that needeth not to be ashamed, rightly dividing the word of truth.
(2nd Timothy 2:15)

When the Word of truth is rightly divided, it sets people free. But so many are held in bondage by what I call sacred cow scriptures. In this chapter we are going to kick over some more of these sacred cows so you can be free to more clearly understand God's Word.

There are always some who say, "Well, yes, I know what you said you believe about the chastening of the Lord. **But what about Job?**"

Well, we're going to find out about Job. The book of Job has been one of the most misunderstood books of the whole Bible. I know; for years it held me in bondage.

Have You Thought You Were Another Job?

Several years ago, when I was going through some financial and physical problems, I stayed up all night reading the book of Job. I was so sure I was another Job, until I had to find out how it turned out. I was both disappointed and thrilled when I got to the end and found out God gave Job twice what he had before.

It thrilled me when I realized it wasn't God who took Job's possessions. Religious people had lied to me. They told me God did it. But, thank God, He didn't.

God Had Put A Hedge About Job.

1 There was a man in the land of Uz, whose name was Job; and that man was perfect and upright, and one that feared God, and eschewed evil.

2 And there were born unto him seven sons and three daughters.

3 His substance also was seven thousand sheep, and three thousand camels, and five hundred yoke of oxen, and five hundred she asses, and a very great household; so that this man was the greatest of all the men of the east.

6 Now there was a day when the sons of God came to present themselves before the Lord, and Satan came also among them.

7 And the Lord said unto Satan, Whence comest thou? Then Satan answered the Lord, and said, From going to and fro in the earth, and from walking up and down in it.

8 And the Lord said unto Satan, Hast thou considered my ser-

vant Job, that there is none like him in the earth, a perfect and
an upright man, one that feareth God, and escheweth evil?

9 Then Satan answered the Lord, and said, Doth Job fear God
for nought?

10 Hast not thou made an hedge about him, and about his house,
and about all that he hath on every side? thou has blessed the
work of his hands, and his substance is increased in the land.

11 But put forth thine hand now, and touch all that he hath, and
he will curse thee to thy face.

12 And the Lord said unto Satan, Behold, all that he hath is in
thy power; only upon himself put not forth thine hand. So Satan
went forth from the presence of the Lord. (Job 1:1-3,6-12)

Fear Broke The Hedge.

Verse twelve is where so many people miss it. Most people interpret it this way: Well, God turned Job over to the
devil.

But now wait a minute. They read that between the lines.
It's not in the Bible. Here it says God said, *Behold, all that
he hath is in thy power,* or **in your hand.** God didn't put
him in the devil's hands. He was **already** there. God didn't
pull the hedge down, Job did, with fear.

4 And his sons went and feasted in their houses, every one his
day; and sent and called for their three sisters to eat and to drink
with them.

5 And it was so, when the days of their feasting were gone about,
that Job sent and sanctified them, and rose up early in the morning, and offered burnt offerings according to the number of them
all: for Job said, It may be that my sons have sinned, and cursed
God in their hearts. **Thus did Job continually.** (Job 1:4-5)

Job Continually Offered Sacrifices.

Here it says Job did this continually. Job was **afraid** that something bad was going to happen to his children. He was always offering these sacrifices; always worrying; always in a turmoil about it.

God didn't put Job in Satan's hands. Job's fear put him in Satan's power. It wasn't something that God did at all.

But so many read that in there. This is why it's so very important that we renew our minds to the Word of God.

When you get your mind renewed to the Word of God, you begin to think like God thinks. Then when you find something in the scripture that is inconsistent with many other scriptures, you know you have the wrong interpretation of it.

Job's Fear Manifest.

Let's examine some of the things that happened to Job.

13 And there was a day when his sons and his daughters were eating and drinking wine in their eldest brother's house:

14 And there came a messenger unto Job, and said, The oxen were plowing, and the asses feeding beside them:

15 And the Sabeans fell upon them, and took them away; yea, they have slain the servants with the edge of the sword; and I only am escaped alone to tell thee.

16 While he was yet speaking, there came also another, and said, The fire of God is fallen from heaven, and hath burned up the sheep, and the servants, and consumed them; and I only am escaped alone to tell thee. (Job 1:13-16)

The King James Version says: "The fire of God" fell from heaven.

But it wasn't the fire of God, it was the work of the devil.

Satan Uses Nature's Elements To Destroy.

A general belief in those days was that everything that happened came from God. Evidently, this was lightning. One translation says lightning. But the ones who reported to Job said it was fire from God.

Lightning is created by atmospheric conditions. Evidently, lightning struck a pond where all of the sheep were watering, and it killed them all.

Just because it came from the sky, that does not mean it was from God. All of these bad things that happened were the work of the devil. The devil brings destruction through storms. This is evident in Mark 4:36-40. For Jesus stopped the storm. It has to be the work of the devil, or else Jesus was destroying the work of His Father.

First John 3:8 says,

> . . . *For this purpose the Son of God was manifested, that he might destroy the works of the devil.* (1st Peter 3:8)

Jesus destroyed the storm. If it were the work of His Father, then Jesus was destroying the work of His Father. So we know the devil started that storm.

Job's Assessment Of His Troubles.

Here in Job one, you have another situation where the elements of nature are causing havoc with Job's property.

19 And, behold, there came a great wind from the wilderness, and smote the four corners of the house, and it fell upon the young men, and they are dead; and I only am escaped alone to tell thee.

20 Then Job arose, and rent his mantle, and shaved his head, and fell down upon the ground, and worshipped,

21 And said, Naked came I out of my mother's womb, and naked shall I return thither: the Lord gave, and the Lord hath taken away; blessed be the name of the Lord. (Job 1:19-21)

If you have ever been to a funeral, you have probably heard this scripture quoted. This was Job's assessment of his troubles. **It is true that Job said it. But what Job said was not the truth.** But yet, Job believed it to be true.

In all this Job sinned not, nor charged God foolishly. (Job 1:22)

Job didn't attribute folly to God. Job didn't do that foolishly, because he really believed what he said was true.

But just because a fellow believes it doesn't necessarily make it so. Here is where so many have become sidetracked from the truth. They have looked at that and said, "Well, the Bible says the Lord gave and the Lord took it away."

But the Bible didn't really say that. Job said that, and the Bible records what Job actually said about his situation. But that does not make it true just because Job said it.

I could tell you that fish have four legs and climb ladders. And you could go tell others that I said fish have four legs, and they climb ladders. You would be truly reporting what I said, but what I said was not true. How many fish have you ever seen climbing a ladder?

28

All Scripture Is Not Inspired Of God.

So it is recorded in the Bible that Job said the Lord gave and the Lord taketh away. But it is not the truth.

Some say, "But the Bible says all scripture is inspired of God, so it must be true."

The Bible didn't really say that. But that's what some say the Bible said. Let's go to Second Timothy three and read it for ourselves.

> *All scripture is given by inspiration of God, and is profitable for doctrine, for reproof, for correction, for instruction in righteousness.* (2nd Timothy 3:16)

If you don't know the difference between what is given by inspiration, and **what is inspired of God,** then you are going to be in trouble soon.

All Scripture Is Given By Inspiration.

When we assume the two statements are the same, we get our thinking all squirreled up.

No, all scripture is **not inspired** of God. All scripture is **given by inspiration** of God. All scripture is profitable. *. . . for doctrine, for reproof. . . . Notice, **all scripture is profitable for reproof, . . . for correction, for instruction in righteousness.***

Job 1:21 is a passage of scripture that is profitable for reproof. Sure, Job said the Lord gave and the Lord hath taken away. But you have to realize, Job couldn't read the first chapter of Job to find out the devil did it.

Yes, *all scripture is given by inspiration of God,* but not all scripture is inspired of God.

29

Ananias And Sapphira Lied.

There are lies recorded in the Bible. Those lies are not inspired of God. Now, I didn't say the Bible lied. I said there are **lies recorded** in the Bible. I'm glad God inspired the writer to record these things in the Bible so that we would know what caused their problems.

Take Ananias and Sapphira, for instance. They saw other people were selling their property and bringing the money to the apostles' feet, so they decided they would pretend to do the same, but hold back part of the price.

1 But a certain man named Ananias, with Sapphira his wife, sold a possession,

2 and kept back part of the price, his wife also being privy to it, and brought a certain part, and laid it at the apostles' feet.

3 But Peter said, Ananias, why hath Satan filled thine heart to lie to the Holy Ghost, and to keep back part of the price of the land? (Acts 5:1-3)

They didn't have to give it all. They didn't have to give any of it. It was theirs. They could do what they wanted with it. But the problem was that they lied to Peter, and to the Holy Ghost, and to God.

God Inspired Writer To Record The Lie.

Peter said,

Whiles it remained, was it not thine own? and after it was sold, was it not in thine own power? why hast thou conceived this thing in thine heart? thou hast not lied unto men but unto God. (Acts 5:4)

The Spirit of God revealed to Peter that they were lying about it.

You see that lie recorded in the Bible. That lie was not inspired of God. But God inspired the writer to record it. And it is profitable for reproof, for rebuke, and instruction.

Job said, *The Lord gave, and the Lord hath taken away.* It's true that Job said that, but what he said was not the truth. Even so, it is true that Ananias and Sapphira said they sold the land for so much. But what they said was not the truth. Yet, God inspired the writer to include that in the scriptures so we could learn from it.

Rightly Dividing The Word.

By rightly dividing the Word, we can say all scripture is profitable for doctrine, for reproof. This verse in Job 1:21 is a scripture that is profitable for reproof.

Here is one verse that I couldn't understand for many years.

In all this Job sinned not, nor charged God foolishly. (Job 1:22)

Up to that point, he hadn't charged God foolishly. But after chapter one, there are 74 different false accusations that Job brought against God. (Dake's Bible lists them.) So if you take this verse, which is a truth, and try to make it the whole truth, you are not rightly dividing the truth. For later, Job did charge God foolishly.

Faith Or Fear Comes By Hearing.

Let's look at some of the things Job said and we will get some insight into how these things started.

31

For the thing which I greatly feared is come upon me, and that which I was afraid of is come unto me. (Job 3:25)

Now let's approach this from a scriptural viewpoint. The Bible says **faith is the substance of things hoped for, the evidence of things not seen. Faith in God comes by hearing the Word of God.** Now that is a positive truth concerning the Word of God.

Reciprocal Truths.

But on the other hand, there is an opposite or reciprocal of that truth, which would be this. Since faith in God comes by hearing the Word of God, then **faith in the devil would come by hearing the words of the devil.**

That's the opposite end of this truth. If you begin to listen to the devil, it will produce fear. Fear is the reverse gear of faith. So if faith is the substance of things desired, then the reciprocal of that truth is that **fear is the substance of things not desired.** Faith cometh by hearing the Word of God. And fear cometh by hearing the words of the devil.

When you rightly divide the Word, you begin to see some reasons why tragedies come to so many people.

If you listen to the devil, you began to believe the things the devil says. Then you begin to speak what you believe. Jesus defeated the devil on the mount, because Jesus never would say anything except what His Father said. The disciples awakened Him in the middle of the storm, with the boat about to sink, when it looked like they were all going to drown, and all He said was "Peace! Be still!"

You Live By God's Word and Die By The Devil's Words.

We need to take note of the fact that on the mount of temptation, Jesus wouldn't say anything other than what His Father said. When tempted to turn stones into bread, he replied,

> *It is written, Man shall not live by bread alone, but by every Word that proceedeth out of the mouth of God.* (Matthew 4:4)

That verse is a truth. But the reciprocal of that truth is this—**if you live by every Word of God, you will die by the words of the devil.** There is a reciprocal to Mark 11:23.

> *Whosoever shall say unto this mountain, Be thou removed, and be thou cast into the sea; and shall not doubt in his heart, but shall believe that those things which he saith shall come to pass; he shall have whatsoever he saith.* (Mark 11:23)

The reciprocal of that is, whosoever shall say to the mountain, "Mountain, you're getting bigger. I'll never get over you," he will have a bigger mountain.

Fear Comes By Hearing.

Then he can't blame it on God when the mountain grows bigger. Neither can you blame God for what happened to Job. Job said out of his own mouth, *the thing which I greatly feared is come upon me, and that which I was afraid of is come unto me.* (Job 3:25) He was speaking his fears.

Fear comes by hearing the words of the devil. The devil lied to Job. The devil told Job that he was going to lose everything he had. Evidently, Job believed it, because when calamity came, the first thing he said was, *Naked came I out of my mother's womb, and naked shall I return.* (Job 1:21) In other words, "I knew it was too good to be true; I was expecting it to happen."

Job's Fear Broke The Hedge—Serpent Bit Him.

Notice what Job said. *the thing I **greatly feared.** . . .* Job didn't just fear. He was highly developed in his fear.

Ecclesiastes 10:8 gives us some insight into Job's situation. . . . *whoso breaketh an hedge, a serpent shall bite him.* Job's fear broke the hedge that God had put about him. Satan's very accusation against God was,

> *Hast not thou made an hedge about him, and about his house, and about all that he hath on every side? thou has blessed the work of his hands, and his substance is increased in the land.* (Job 1:10)

In other words, Satan said, "You have hedged him about until I can't get to him." I can just imagine God standing there grinning, saying, "Yes, that's Me. That's what I did, all right."

God hedged him about on every side, but through fear the hedge came down. So many believe that God took the hedge down. No, God didn't take the hedge down. Ecclesiastes 10:8 hit the nail on the head when it says, *. . .whoso breaketh an hedge, a serpent shall bite him.* Job broke the hedge, and a serpent bit him.

> *25 For the thing which I greatly feared is come upon me, and that which I was afraid of is come unto me.*

26 I was not in safety, neither had I rest, neither was quiet; yet trouble came. (Job 3:25-26)

From these scriptures it seems that Job was worried, was over-wrought, was fretting, and was praying and offering sacrifices—but he had faith in none of them.

You may think I am too hard on Job. But we must rightly divide the Word and let the chips fall where they may. This shows what fear will do to you. If you get to where you can't sleep, you can't rest, you can't believe God— you've been listening to the devil. Let me say it again: faith in God comes by hearing the Word of God. Faith in the devil comes by hearing the words of the devil.

Wisdom Speaks And Gives Insight.

20 Wisdom crieth without; she uttereth her voice in the streets:

21 She crieth in the chief place of concourse, in the openings of the gates: in the city she uttereth her words, saying

22 How long, ye simple ones, will ye love simplicity? and the scorners delight in their scorning, and fools hate knowledge.

23 Turn you at my reproof: behold, I will pour out my spirit unto you, I will make known my words unto you.

24 Because I have called, and ye refused; I have stretched out my hand, and no man regarded;

25 But ye have set at nought all my counsel, and would none of my reproof:

26 I also will laugh at your calamity; I will mock when your fear cometh;

27 When your fear cometh as desolation, and your destruction cometh as a whirlwind; when distress and anguish cometh upon you.

28 Then shall they call upon me, but I will not answer; they shall seek me early, but they shall not find me:

29 For they hated knowledge, and did not choose the fear of the Lord:

30 They would none of my counsel: they despised all my reproof.

31 Therefore shall they eat of the fruit of their own way, and be filled with their own devices.

32 For the turning away of the simple shall slay them, and the prosperity of fools shall destroy them.

*33 **But whoso hearkeneth unto me shall dwell safely, and shall be quiet from fear of evil.*** (Proverbs 1:20-33)

Now notice, this is not God saying, "I won't hear you." But this is Wisdom talking. Wisdom won't come to you when you have operated in your own way. You can't summon wisdom and get it, because you're worrying, you're fretting, you're in fear. It will not come then, for there is no faith for it.

Wisdom says, *But whoso hearkeneth unto me shall dwell safely, and shall be quiet from fear of evil.* (Proverbs 1:33)

Now link this to Proverbs, the third chapter.

21 My son, let not them depart from thine eyes: keep sound wisdom and discretion:

22 So shall they be life unto thy soul, and grace to thy neck.

23 Then shalt thou walk in thy way safely, and thy foot shall not stumble.

24 When thou liest down, thou shalt not be afraid: yea, thou shalt lie down, and thy sleep shall be sweet.

25 Be not afraid of sudden fear, neither of the desolation of the wicked, when it cometh.

26 For the Lord shall be thy confidence, and shall keep thy foot from being taken. (Proverbs 3:21-26)

Remember, Job said, *I was not in safety, neither had I rest.* He said, *The thing which I greatly feared is come upon me.*

Fear Is The Substance Of Trouble.

The more highly developed you are in either fear or faith, the quicker the manifestation will come. Just as faith is the substance of **things desired,** fear is the substance of **things not desired.** On almost every occasion that Jesus appeared to His disciples after He arose from the dead, He said, "Fear not!"

On another occasion, Jesus said, *Let not your heart be troubled; neither be afraid.*

Let's go to Job, chapter six.

. . .Deliver me from the enemy's hand? or, Redeem me from the hand of the mighty? (Job 6:23)

Notice, Job is saying, *Deliver me from the enemy's hand.* Now **he has figured it out it's the devil**, and not God who's calling him "the mighty."

Look at verse 24.

Teach me, and I will hold my tongue: and cause me to understand wherein I have erred. (Job 6:24)

Now he found out his tongue had something to do with it. So he has admitted, "I've missed it somewhere." Then he says, *How forcible are right words!. . .* (v 25) So he is convinced that words had something to do with it.

Job admitted the thing he greatly feared had come upon him, saying, *I was not in safety, neither had I rest. Yet trouble came.*

Yet Proverbs says, if you trust in the Lord, when you lie down, your sleep would be sweet, and you would be quiet from fear of evil.

Job Spoke Things He Didn't Understand.

Now let's go to the forty-second chapter of Job.

1 Then Job answered the Lord, and said,

2 I know that thou canst do every thing, and that no thought can be withholden from thee.

3 Who is he that hideth counsel without knowledge? therefore have I uttered that I understood not; things too wonderful for me, which I knew not.

4 Hear, I beseech thee, and I will speak: I will demand of thee, and declare thou unto me.

5 I have heard of thee by the hearing of the ear: but not mine eye seeth thee.

6 Wherefore I abhor myself, and repent in dust and ashes (Job 42:1-6)

Here Job admits, "I have uttered things that I did not understand."

In other words, he said, "I flat missed it. But I've learned some things that I didn't know."

Then notice what God said to Job's comforters.

Therefore take unto you now seven bullocks and seven rams, and go to my servant Job, and offer up for yourselves a burnt offering; and my servant Job shall pray for you:

38

for him will I accept: lest I deal with you after your folly, in that ye have not spoken of me the thing which is right, like my servant Job. (Job 42:8)

Job's comforters had missed it just as much as Job had, but they wouldn't admit it.

Job's Captivity Turned.

And the Lord turned the captivity of Job, when he prayed for his friends: also the Lord gave Job twice as much as he had before. (Job 42:10)

God has been accused of doing many things to Job. But this is what God really did to Job.

You will notice verse 10 says, *the LORD turned the captivity of Job. . . .* For a clearer understanding of Job's plight, ask yourself this. **If the Lord turned his captivity, who had him captive?**

We know God did not have him captive. Then **it had to be the devil.** When the Lord turned his captivity, this indicates that after the turning, then Job had the devil captive. This came about because Job prayed for his enemies. I know the Bible says, "friends," but **with friends like that, you sure don't need any enemies.** I believe God was calling things that are not when He called them Job's friends.

Have you noticed that most people never talk about the things God gave Job? They usually talk about what they thought God took away from him.

But God was not the taker. He is the giver of all good gifts. Job allowed himself to be ensnared by the devil because fear broke the hedge. Paul says in Second Timothy

2:26 that we must recover ourselves out of the snare of the devil.

We are all subject to missing it. It's not a crime to miss it, but there comes a time when we must admit we've been wrong. Allow me to paraphrase what Job said: "I just flat missed it, and I've uttered things, But I didn't know what I was talking about, and I repent." And God gave him twice as much as the devil stole from him.

But the predominant thing we hear about all of Job's problems is what he said **before** he realized the devil caused it: *The Lord gave, and the Lord hath taken away.* You must realize that was only Job's assessment of the situation at first. But in chapter six he said, "deliver me from the enemy's hand." It took him a while to understand that it was in fact the devil who took away.

We can learn some valuable lessons from Job's experience. This is why the Bible says, *all scripture is given by inspiration of God, and is profitable for doctrine, for reproof, for correction, for instruction in righteousness.* (2nd Timothy 3:1)

God is a good God. The devil is a bad enemy. We also need to understand that there are some things that happened under the old covenant that won't happen under the new covenant.

For one thing, under the old covenant there was no intercessor. **God had no man** to stand in the gap and **make up the hedge** that had been broken. But we have a man today. **Jesus our intercessor.**

Chapter 3

OTHERS OF
HEBREWS ELEVEN

Now faith is the substance of things hoped for, the evidence of things not seen. (Hebrews 11:1)

We all know that the eleventh chapter of Hebrews is what we call the "Hall of Faith." It talks about all of the great patriarchs who did great things through faith, and brought forth a manifestation of God's power in the earth through faith. It names Abel, Enoch, Noah, Abraham, Isaac, Jacob, Joseph, Moses, Joshua, Rahab, Gideon, Barak, Samson, Jephthae, David, and Samuel as heroes of faith. We will pick it up in verse 33.

33 Who through faith subdued kingdoms, wrought righteousness, obtained promises, stopped the mouths of lions,

34 Quenched the violence of fire, escaped the edge of the sword, out of weakness were made strong, waxed valiant in fight, turned to flight the armies of the aliens.

35 Women received their dead raised to life again: and others were tortured, not accepting deliverance: that they might obtain a better resurrection;

*36 And **others had trial of cruel mockings and scourgings, yea, moreover of bonds and imprisonment:***

*37 **They were stoned, they were sawn asunder, were tempted, were slain with the sword: they wandered about in sheepskins and goatskins; being destitute, afflicted, tormented;***

*38 **(Of whom the world was not worthy:) they wandered in deserts, and in mountains, and in dens and caves of the earth.***

*39 **And these all, having obtained a good report through faith, received not the promise.*** (Hebrews 11:33-39)

This is what we are referring to as the "others" of Hebrews eleven. So many read these passages and say, "Well, I heard what you're teaching about faith and the power of God to deliver from every situation. But look at what happened to the "others" of Hebrews eleven. Some were sawn asunder, some didn't get delivered, some didn't come out victorious.

Pity Parties Are Not The Answer.

You need to know why some of these things happen. When they face problems in life, many people want to go to these scriptures and have a pity party. They say, "Well, these people were sawn asunder, and some were tortured and were not delivered, so I guess this must be the will of God for me."

It's in times of trouble that people want to have pity parties, and feel sorry for themselves.

Usually, you can take a person's Bible, thumb through it and by taking note of the scriptures they have underlined, pretty well tell what they believe. People who are always feeling sorry for themselves, always in problems and troubles and trials, **will have all of the suffering scriptures underlined in their Bible**. They will have all of the scriptures underlined where Paul was beaten, and stoned, and in jail. They want to identify with suffering, instead of identifying with victory.

We need to realize it is God's will that we live victoriously in life, regardless of what happened to the "others" of Hebrews eleven.

Faith — The Substance Of Things Desired.

Let's go to the book of Hebrews and work our way through the whole eleventh chapter. We're going to pick up on some other scriptures as well, that will give insight into the others of Hebrews eleven.

1 Now faith is the substance of things hoped for, the evidence of things not seen.

2 For by it the elders obtained a good report.

3 Through faith we understand that the worlds were framed by the word of God, so that things which are seen were not made of things which do appear.

4 By faith Abel offered unto God a more excellent sacrifice than Cain, by which he obtained witness that he was righteous, God testifying of his gifts: and by it he being dead yet speaketh. (Hebrews 11:1-4)

Faith And Problems.

Here the writer begins to tell you of those who operated in overcoming faith.

Remember, just because you get turned on to faith, that doesn't mean you will never have any more problems in life. You are going to have some problems in life. But thank God, you can have victory over those problems by holding fast to the Word of God and walking in the light of the scriptures.

You can find that Abel had some problems **because of his faith.** His sacrifice was received because of his faith. ***By faith Abel offered unto God a more excellent sacrifice than Cain.*** Abel's faith got him in trouble.

Abel didn't have the promises that we have today. The new covenant is established on better promises.

Enoch's Private Rapture.

By faith Enoch was translated that he should not see death; and was not found, because God had translated him: for before his translation he had this testimony, that he pleased God. (Hebrews 11:5)

Here is a man who lived so close to God, and was highly developed in his faith, even under the old covenant. By faith he was translated.

Enoch had his own private rapture, even though it was

not for that dispensation. The rapture is for another dispensation altogether. But here is a man who by faith looked down through the eons of time and said, "Well, I'll just take my rapture now."

He was able through faith to reach out beyond his dispensation to bring into manifestation something that was not even for that age.

I am convinced that through faith, through the wisdom and direction of the Holy Spirit, it is possible to reach into the millennium age and bring into our generation some things that are to come forth during the millennium—especially inventions that will help usher in the millennium on the earth. Faith is the substance of those things that are not yet seen.

Pleasing God Is Impossible Without Faith.

6 But without faith it is impossible to please him: for he that cometh to God must believe that he is, and that he is a rewarder of them that diligently seek him.

7 By faith Noah, being warned of God of things not seen as yet, moved with fear, prepared an ark to the saving of his house; by the which he condemned the world, and became heir of the righteousness which is by faith.

8 By faith Abraham, when he was called to go out into a place which he should after receive for an inheritance, obeyed; and he went out, not knowing whither he went.

9 By faith he sojourned in the land. . .
11 Through faith also Sara herself received strength to conceive seed, and was delivered of a child when she was past age, because she judged him faithful who had promised. (Hebrews 11:6-9,11)

All of these things happened because of faith.

Sara received a promise from God, she received hope from that promise, and she believed that promise. She didn't have the new covenant as we have it today. But she had God's Word concerning her, and she believed it. When there was no hope naturally, Abraham decided to believe in hope, that he might become the father of many nations. *Through faith also Sara herself received strength to conceive seed.*

> *12 Therefore sprang there even of one, and him as good as dead, so many as the stars of the sky in multitude, and as the sand which is by the sea shore innumerable.*
>
> *13 These all died in faith, not having received the promises, but having seen them afar off, and were persuaded of them, and embraced them, and confessed that they were strangers and pilgrims on the earth.* (Hebrews 11:12-13)

Don't Be Caught Dead Without Faith.

A certain person wrote me a letter and said, "I know what you're teaching, that through faith you can be healed. But our pastor said that faith couldn't have anything to do with healing because the scripture says these people all died in faith."

Well, that brother is either unlearned in the scriptures or he's dishonest. For the promise referred to here is the promise of the Messiah, and the promise that God made to Abraham about his seed becoming as the sand of the sea.

Acts, chapter seven gives us some insight into this.

> *But when the time of the promise drew nigh, which God had sworn to Abraham, the people grew and multiplied in Egypt.* (Acts 7:17)

46

Notice the phrase, *when the time of the promise grew nigh*. The promise God made to Abraham could not have happened in his day. It was an impossibility for all the promises to have been consummated in the day that Abraham lived. For one of the promises was that his seed was going to be as the sand upon the seashore and as the stars of the heavens—innumerable. This couldn't have happened in his lifetime. So it's wrong for an individual to say that Hebrews 11:13 proves that faith doesn't have anything to do with obtaining the promises of God because it says these all died in faith.

You surely don't ever want to be caught dead without faith. Sure they died in faith, *but having seen them afar off.*

The context of this is referring to the fact that they did perceive these things as future events.

Faith To Obtain Promises.

Some see the promises in the new covenant—which are for us today—afar off. But the new covenant is our "promised land," just as God told the children of Israel, "I've given you the land; go in and possess it." It belonged to them. It was theirs. It was God's will for them to possess it.

The scriptures say the Word was preached to us as well as unto them, but the Word preached **did not profit them** because they wouldn't mix any faith with it. So if we say, "Well, yes I know the Bible says my God will meet my need according to His riches in glory, but I guess that means when we get to heaven," then we're not seeing this promise in the now. We are seeing it afar off.

But faith is always in the now. The scripture says, ***Now*** *faith is the substance of things hoped for.* It's **now faith.** That's the kind of faith we're talking about—present tense faith. The apostle Paul said all the promises of God are Yes and Amen. In other words, God has already said Yes to all the promises in the new covenant. The New Testament is the **last will and testament of our Lord Jesus Christ.**

Faith For Inheritance.

If your rich uncle wrote you in his will and you were to receive all of his possessions as your inheritance, would you think you were going to receive that when you died?

No, you wouldn't receive it after **you** died. You would receive it after **he** died.

So many believers have been deceived into believing they are going to receive their inheritance after **they** die.

But we are joint heirs with Jesus. A testament is in force after the testator has died. When he dies, then you receive the inheritance—not when you die.

Well, Jesus has already died, and we have received our promised inheritance. But in order to enforce the will, we must mix faith with those promises. What would we think about an individual who said, "Well, my rich uncle has willed all of his land, all of his riches to me. He has millions of dollars worth of investments, and it will be all mine! Oh, I just can hardly wait until I die so I can get this inheritance!"

You would want to know where he went to school.

Well, we've been thinking that way for years when it comes to our spiritual inheritance. The devil has conned

48

us into believing that our inheritance is afar off. But our inheritance became available when Jesus died—not when we die.

We Are No More Strangers But Citizens.

Now back to Hebrews eleven, where it says, *These all died in faith, not having received the promises, but having seen them afar off, and were persuaded of them, and embraced them, and confessed that they were strangers and pilgrims on the earth. (v.13)* This is what they confessed under the old covenant. But we have a better covenant, and it is established on better promises.

> *Now therefore ye are no more strangers and foreigners, but fellow citizens with the saints, and of the household of God.* (Ephesians 2:19)

Because of what Jesus did, we are no more strangers or foreigners, but fellow citizens. Our citizenship is of heaven now. Romans 8:17 tells us we are joint heirs of Christ. So we have it much better under the new covenant.

Abraham Validates The Covenant.

> *By faith Abraham, when he was tried, offered up Isaac: and he that had received the promises offered up his only begotten son.* (Hebrews 11:17)

God required Abraham to offer his son Isaac—and this bothered me for years. I would say, "Why in the world would God ask Abraham to kill his own son?" This was the very thing that made the blood covenant valid forever.

God asked Abraham for his son. This covenant that He made with Abraham was so strong, so powerful that it meant, whatever you have, Abraham, belongs to me—even to your life, if I require it. When God said, "Go sacrifice your only son, the promised child," Abraham didn't question that, because he knew the covenant.

God was requiring Abraham to validate that covenant to prove to the whole universe that Abraham could and would keep the covenant. A covenant between two people is no good unless it is signed by both parties. God has sworn by Himself that He would perform His oath. But what was Abraham going to do? God knew that Satan was going to challenge Him on this covenant with Abraham by saying, "You made a covenant with a man who can't possibly keep it." So before it ever was challenged, God called on Abraham to prove this covenant valid.

17 By faith Abraham, when he was tried, offered up Isaac and he that had received the promises offered up his only begotten son,

18 Of whom it was said, that in Isaac shall thy seed be called:

19 Accounting that God was able to raise him up, even from the dead; from whence also he received him in a figure. (Hebrews 11:17-19)

In other words, God received Isaac as though he were sacrificed when Abraham raised the knife to kill him.

If Abraham would not offer his son Isaac, then it would be illegal for God to offer His Son as a sacrifice for mankind. But because Abraham was obedient to the covenant—he validated that blood covenant, and it was stamped VALID and it will stand up forever. This was all done by faith.

Hall Of Faith.

20 By faith Isaac blessed Jacob and Esau concerning things to come.

21 By faith Jacob, when he was a dying, blessed both the sons of Joseph; and worshipped, leaning upon the top of his staff.

22 By faith Joseph . . .

23 By faith Moses . . .

29 By faith they passed through the Red sea . . .

30 By faith the walls of Jericho fell down . . .

31 By faith the harlot Rahab perished not with them that believed not . . .

32 And what shall I more say? for the time would fail me to tell of Gideon, and of Barak, and of Samson, and of Jephthae; of David also, and Samuel, and of the prophets:

33 Who through faith subdued kingdoms, wrought righteousness, obtained promises, stopped the mouths of lions,

34 Quenched the violence of fire, escaped the edge of the sword, out of weakness were made strong, waxed valiant in fight, turned to flight the armies of the aliens.

35 Women received their dead raised to life again: and others were tortured, not accepting deliverance; that they might obtain a better resurrection:

36 And others had cruel mockings and scourgings, yea, moreover of bonds and imprisonment:

37 They were stoned, they were sawn asunder, were slain with the sword: they wandered about in sheepskins and goatskins; being destitute, afflicted, tormented. (Hebrews 11:20-23,29-37)

These are the "others" of Hebrews eleven.

Someone said, "Well, what about these others? Why did all of this happen to the others? Why were they not delivered?

God Makes Way Of Escape.

Let me point out a few ways of escape. First Corinthians, the tenth chapter will answer some of these questions. I want you to notice what the apostle Paul says concerning temptations and trials that come your way in life.

> *There hath no temptation taken you but such as is common to man: but God is faithful, who will not suffer you to be tempted above that ye are able; but will with the temptation also make a way to escape, that ye may be able to bear it.* (1st Corinthians 10:13)

We hear this verse quoted this way: "God won't **put** any more on you that you are not able to stand."

But that was not what the apostle Paul said.

Temptation Must Be Common To Man.

12 Wherefore let him that thinketh he standeth take heed lest he fall.

3 There hath no temptation taken you but such as is common to man: but God is faithful, who will not suffer you to be tempted above that ye are able; but will with the temptation also make a way to escape, that ye may be able to bear it. (1st Corinthians 10:12-13)

Paul is saying **Satan cannot tempt you supernaturally. He has to tempt you by that which is common to man. He can't come with some supernatural temptation. He has to come to you through the five physical senses. Satan is limited in his methods of temptation.**

Our Weapons Are Not Carnal.

Paul also said the weapons of our warfare are not carnal but they are mighty through God. So we as believers have the advantage of supernatural weapons. But Satan's temptation is limited to the carnal things. So temptation is only through things that are *common to man: but God is faithful, who will not suffer you to be tempted above that ye are able;* **but will with the temptation also make a way to escape, that ye may be able to bear it.** (1st Corinthians 10:13)

Satan Is The Tempter And Destroyer.

Did you notice that **Paul did not say God sent the temptation?** So many interpret this to mean that God sent the temptation or the trial. But as you read the fourth chapter of Mark, you find that Jesus said it was Satan bringing the trials and the afflictions of life.

John 10:10 is the dividing line of the Bible.

The thief cometh not, but for to steal, and to kill, and to destroy: I am come that they might have life, and that they might have it more abundantly. (John 10:10)

This is the assessment that Jesus made of good and evil. Jesus is the One Who brought life more abundantly, and all things pertaining to it. But the thief comes to kill, steal, and destroy.

Balance Wheel Of The Bible.

So John 10:10 is the dividing line of the Bible. It's the balance wheel of the whole Bible. If you will get a clear understanding of John 10:10, then it will answer many of the questions you have about the things that you face in life.

Paul said, *there hath no temptation taken you but such as is common to man.* God will with any temptation *also make a way to escape, that ye may be able to bear it.* (The word "bear" means to remain.)

If that be true, then why was it then the others of Hebrews eleven didn't bear it?

These are valid questions. I am posing these questions so you will think about it, for sometimes we get indoctrinated and quit thinking. The apostle Paul has brought up something that you need to understand: **God has made a way of escape.**

I realize this is in the New Testament, but I see evidence of this truth in the Old Testament. God delivered Daniel from the lion's den. But what about the others who were eaten by lions? If what the apostle Paul says was true in the old covenant, then there was a way of escape, but they either didn't find it, or they decided not to take the way of escape.

A Way Of Escape Missed Or Ignored.

But God makes a way of escape, that you may be able to bear it. The Greek word "bear" means to remain. But as you read verse 37 of Hebrews eleven, you find out some of them did not remain. It is God's will that we remain in His service until we fulfill His work on earth. God doesn't get glory out of us just giving up our lives for the cause. He gets glory when we overcome the enemy.

As someone so aptly put it, "You don't win a war by giving your life for your country. You win a war by getting your enemies to give their lives."

So the apostle Paul made some statements that we need to look into more thoroughly.

Samson Reaped Wages Of Sin.

Let's look at some of those who were tortured, stoned, and killed by the sword. Let's look at Samson, for instance. He was mightily anointed of God. He took the jawbone of a donkey and slew a thousand men when the anointing came on him. Now you know that was not natural strength. It was supernatural. God had specially anointed him. And God's anointing and calling are without repentance.

Some of the things that Samson did was surely not anointed. But even when Samson was in sin, there was still a supernatural strength that would come upon him. He went to a harlot's house, and as he was leaving about midnight, the enemy had locked the gates to try to capture him. The anointing was upon him so strongly that he pulled up the gates, and he carried the gates and the posts to the top of the hill.

Here was a man who was walking in sin. But still that anointing was operating in his life. I want to point this out to you, because this will help you understand some things you see today. Just because there are miracles and the anointing of God upon an individual, that does not mean God is in favor of everything they are doing. That does not mean they are perfect. When God calls a person and anoints them, even if there are mighty miracles happening in their ministry, that doesn't necessarily mean everything they do is right. That doesn't even mean they are living right. For here in Judges the sixteenth chapter, Samson is a classic example of God's mercy and grace. He was in sin, yet that anointing still came upon him.

Samson Told God's Secret.

Here's the point I'm coming to: why were some of the others of Hebrews eleven tortured? Samson is one who was tortured. In Judges sixteen you find, after he had told God's secret of his anointing, they cut his hair and he lost that anointing, and they bound him. They tortured him and put his eyes out. Then they took him and put him to grinding in the prison house.

That was torture. He is one of the others of Hebrews eleven who suffered and did not remain to bear it.

Samson Did Not Choose Way Of Escape.

In this particular case, Samson suffered and was tortured and died because of his disobedience and sin.

There are some who say, "I just don't understand why God allowed those things to happen to those people."

God didn't have anything to do with it. God made a way of escape. Obedience was Samson's way of escape. He chose not to take it. Samson disobeyed God. He was disobedient to God's will and purpose, his calling and anointing in life. So it caused him much torture, much trouble; it even cost him his life.

God Is Merciful.

But yet, in all of that, God still used him. So you see, even though people do get messed up in life, God will still use them. That doesn't mean God is condoning what they did. Certainly, God didn't condone some of the things that Samson did. It wasn't God's will for Samson to die before his time.

Some of you can think of people in your lifetime who had mighty miracles happening in their ministry; great healing campaigns, and then they died of some sickness or disease. But that wasn't the will of God for them. They missed it somewhere. So many people say, "Well, I just don't understand why this happened to others, or to the others of Hebrews eleven. . . ."

Since God will with any temptation, test, or trial that comes, make a way of escape, then either they didn't find it or they decided not to take it.

We have to look at these things in the light of that scripture in order to understand it. There are also some promises involved here in the new covenant that they did not have under the old covenant.

Solomon's Assessment Of Life.

To get some insight into some things that happened under the old covenant, let's go to Ecclesiastes, chapter four and get Solomon's assessment of life under the old covenant.

> *So I returned, and considered all the oppressions that are done under the sun: and behold the tears of such as were oppressed, and they had no comforter; and on the side of their oppressors there was power; but they had no comforter.* (Ecclesiastes 4:1)

Do you realize what he is talking about here? They didn't have the Holy Spirit, Who is our comforter and guide. Under the old covenant they didn't have a comforter. They didn't have one called alongside to help, to teach them all things.

The oppressor had power, but those who were oppressed didn't have any power, because they didn't have a comforter.

> *2 Wherefore I praised the dead which are already dead more than the living which are yet alive.*
>
> *3 Yea, better is he than both they, which hath not yet been, who hath not seen the evil work that is done under the sun* (Ecclesiastes 4:2-3)

After his statement in verse one, he sums the whole thing up by saying, "You would really be better off dead than alive under this situation."

Then after thinking about it, he said, "You would really be better off if you had never been born than to have been born and died."

He is talking about being under the old covenant. There was power on the side of the oppressor. But those who were oppressed had no comforter nor helper, because there was not one called alongside to help.

New Covenant Established On Better Promises.

This brings us to something we need to consider about these people who suffered and were tortured under the old covenant. They had no comforter. Remember what the new covenant says concerning the Holy Spirit. When He, the Spirit of truth is come, He will guide you into all truth. He will show you things to come.

> *13 Howbeit when he, the Spirit of truth, is come, he will guide you into all truth: for he shall not speak of himself; but what-soever he shall hear, that shall he speak: and he will shew you things to come.*
>
> *15 All things that the Father hath are mine: therefore said I, that he shall take of mine, and shall shew it unto you. (John 16:13,15)*

God has made a way of escape, that we may be able to escape or to bear the situations of life, and the Holy Spirit will reveal it to you so that you will be able to escape.

But under the old covenant they didn't have a comforter. They couldn't call upon this promise that we have under the new covenant.

Under the old covenant, the Holy Spirit came upon only the prophet, the priest, and the king. There were a few exceptions, such as with Mary. But that was an exception, rather than the rule. The average layman did not have access to the Holy Spirit in those days. Then you can understand why the people under the old covenant had such a hard time of it.

Solomon was the wisest man who ever lived, other than Jesus. And he said, "I have considered these things, and you'd be better off dead than alive, for the enemy has power. And those who are oppressed don't have the ability to resist him."

The Curse Of The Law.

Have you ever noticed that in the Old Testament little is said about the devil and his power? There wasn't much they could do about it under the old covenant. If they stayed under the umbrella of that covenant God made with them, (the Book of the Law) then they had divine protection. But once they got out from under that umbrella of protection, then they were legal game for Satan, and they had no power to overcome him. This was the curse of the law. Once they got under that curse of breaking the law, the curses came like a flood. There was no power in the law to make them overcomers.

Power And Authority To Resist The Devil.

But under the new covenant we're redeemed from the curse of the law. (Galatians 3:13) Also, under the new covenant we have authority to use the Name above all names, the name of Jesus. We now can resist the devil and he will flee from us. For there is power in that Name.

So you can understand why Solomon said, "I have considered this whole thing and have decided that you'd be better off dead than living under our situation." God was not pleased with the old covenant. So He changed it to a better covenant. Solomon was right, and God changed it.

Thank God He did change it. There is a comforter today! There is an intercessor today!

The others of Hebrews eleven had no intercessor. It makes a difference when you have an intercessor—someone who can stand in the gap and make up the hedge.

This will explain to you why some of the others of Hebrews eleven were sawn asunder. It wasn't because it was God's will for that to happen to them. For there was a way some of those things could have been avoided.

Some of these people who were sawn asunder, some of these who died, becoming martyrs for the gospel, went beyond the call of duty. It may not have been required of them, but they considered what they were doing so important that they did it anyway. And through their faith they pleased God.

Chapter 4

SOME ESCAPED.
OTHERS DIDN'T.

In this chapter we are continuing on the subject of the "others" of Hebrews eleven—those who were stoned, those who were sawn asunder, those who were slain by the sword.

So many people want to relate to these others of Hebrews eleven. They seem to ignore those,

> *33 Who through faith subdued kingdoms, wrought righteousness, obtained promises, stopped the mouths of lions,*
>
> *34 Quenched the violence of fire, escaped the edge of the sword, out of weakness were made strong, waxed valiant in flight turned to flight the armies of the aliens.* (Hebrews 11:33-34)

We must realize that some things happened under the old covenant which will not happen under the new covenant, if we appropriate the promises.

Power Of The Oppressor.

Remember, Solomon said you'd be better off if you had never been born, than to have been born and died under the old covenant. For there was power on the side of the oppressor, but there was no power on the side of those who were oppressed, **because they had no comforter.**

Revelation For The Believer Today.

Let's look at some of the promises of the New Testament. We will begin in John, the fourteenth chapter, where Jesus is speaking.

16 And I will pray the Father, and he shall give you another Comforter, that he may abide with you for ever;

17 Even the Spirit of truth; whom the world cannot receive, because it seeth him not, neither knoweth him: but ye know him; for he dwelleth with you, and shall be in you. (John 14:16-17)

The Spirit of truth was the Spirit of Christ. In other words, He is saying, **I am coming back to get inside you in the person of the Holy Spirit, to give you power, to be your Comforter, and to be your guide.**

I will not leave you comfortless: I will come to you. (John 14:18)

12 I have yet many things to say unto you, but ye cannot bear them now.

13 Howbeit when he, the Spirit of truth, is come. . . . (John 16:12-13)

Jesus said, "You can't bear these things now." There were some things that the people under the old covenant—

people who were oppressed—could not understand. They did not have the knowledge that we have under the new covenant.

> *13 Howbeit when he, the Spirit of truth, is come, he will guide you into all truth: for he shall not speak of himself; but whatsoever he shall hear, that shall he speak: and he will shew you things to come.*
>
> *14 He shall glorify me: for he shall receive of mine, and shall shew it unto you.*
>
> *15 All things that the Father hath are mine: therefore said I, that he shall take of mine, and shall shew it unto you.* (John 16:13-15)

This is God's direction to us under the new covenant. But in Ecclesiastes, the fourth chapter, Solomon says there was no comforter. There was none to teach the truth and the understanding. There was none to fill in the gap and make up the edge.

Some of these things of Hebrews eleven could have been avoided if they had the Holy Spirit to reveal their way of escape. But they didn't have a comforter. They did not have the Holy Spirit. They did not have the name of Jesus.

Authority Over The Devil.

We find scriptures in the new covenant that **give us power and authority over the devil.** In Luke ten, Jesus said to the disciples,

> *Behold, I give unto you power to tread on serpents and scorpions, and over all the power of the enemy: and nothing shall by any means hurt you.* (Luke 10:19)

Under the old covenant, the Holy Ghost came upon only the prophet, the priest, and the king. But now, under the new covenant, there is power on the side of those who are the target of the oppressor. The tables have been turned. And today, under the new covenant, we have the advantage. Satan's temptation is limited to that which is common to man. But the weapons of our warfare are not carnal. We have supernatural weapons they didn't have under the old covenant.

No Man To Stand In The Gap.

30 And I sought for a man among them, that should make up the hedge, and stand in the gap before me for the land, that I should not destroy it: but I found none.

31 Therefore have I poured out mine indignation upon them; I have consumed them with the fire of my wrath: their own way have I recompensed upon their heads, saith the Lord God. (Ezekiel 22:30-31)

God sought for a man to stand in the gap and make up the hedge. On one occasion, Moses stood between God and Israel. (Allow me to paraphrase.) God said, "I will wipe them out and I will make a great nation from you."

Moses said, "Oh, no you won't!"

Moses stood up to God, saying, "God, you can't do that because of Your Word."

He reminded God of what He said. And God said, "You're right. I won't do it."

Moses stood in the gap for Israel.

9 Therefore is judgment far from us, neither doth justice over-take us: we wait for light, but behold obscurity; for brightness, but we walk in darkness.

10 We grope for the wall like the blind, and we grope as if we had no eyes: we stumble at noon day as in the night; we are in desolate places as dead men.

11 We roar all like bears, and mourn sore like doves: we look for judgment, but there is none; for salvation, but it is far off from us.

12 For our transgressions are multiplied before thee, and our sins testify against us: for our transgressions are with us; and as for our iniquities, we know them.

13 In transgressing and lying against the Lord, and departing away from our God, speaking oppression and revolt, conceiv-ing and uttering from the heart words of falsehood.

14 And judgment is turned away backward, and justice standeth afar off: for truth is fallen in the street, and equity cannot enter.

15 Yea, truth faileth; and he that departeth from evil maketh himself a prey: and the Lord saw it, and it displeased him that there was no judgment. (Isaiah 59:9-15)

Now remember, what is being said here is under the old covenant, when there was no remission of sins. There was only an atonement or a covering for sin. The sin was still there. They were still conscious of their sin. Only under the new covenant does the blood of Jesus take away the consciousness of sin.

God is making a statement similar to that of Solomon. He said this thing is out of balance. This should not be, because *truth faileth; and he that departeth from evil maketh himself prey.* In other words, he said those who say they are going to depart from evil become a prey to the devil.

And he saw that there was no man, and wondered that there was no intercessor: therefore his arm brought salvation unto him; and his righteousness, it sustained him. (Isaiah 59:16)

God said, "We are going to do something about it, for this is not right."

He saw that there was no man, and wondered that there was no intercessor. . . . Solomon said there was no "comforter."

Our Intercessor Has Come.

Let's go to First John, the second chapter.

My little children, these things write I unto you, that ye sin not. And if any man sin, we have an advocate with the Father, Jesus Christ the righteous. (1st John 2:1)

That word "advocate" is very important, because it actually means "intercessor." We have an intercessor. Romans 8:34 tells us Jesus is *at the right hand of God, who also maketh intercession for us.* Hebrews 7:25 says of Jesus, *he ever liveth to make intercession for them.*

For the others of Hebrews eleven, there was no intercessor. There was no man to stand in the gap and make up the hedge.

But now we have a man. His name is Jesus. He is our intercessor.

This will answer many of your questions about why things happened as they did under the old covenant. Many are confused when they read the old covenant and see the things that happened there. They say, "I just don't understand why God allowed these things to happen."

Don't Blame God For Man's Mistakes.

When you check into it, as we did concerning Samson, you find that some of those things happened to them because of their sin.

David also caused some of his own problems. He suffered **some things** because of his sin. It wasn't the will of God for many of those things to happen. Sin brought it upon these people.

Let's continue with Isaiah fifty-nine.

16 And he saw that there was no man, and wondered that there was no intercessor: therefore his arm brought salvation unto him; and his righteousness, it sustained him.

17 For he put on righteousness as a breastplate, and an helmet of salvation upon his head; and he put on the garments of vengeance for clothing, and was clad with zeal as a cloak.

18 According to their deeds, accordingly he will repay, fury to his adversaries, recompence to his enemies; to the islands he will repay recompence.

19 . . . when the enemy shall come in like a flood, the spirit of the Lord shall lift up a standard against him. (Isaiah 59:16-19)

A Flood Can't Be Contained.

*. . . **When the enemy shall come in like a flood, the Spirit of the Lord shall lift up a standard against him.*** (Isaiah 59:19)

Notice the way this is punctuated in the King James Bible: **when the enemy shall come in like a flood, [then] the spirit of the Lord shall lift up a standard against him.**

This is the way I had always looked at this verse, until

69

a minister friend, Billy Rash, asked, "have you ever stopped to consider that **a flood is something you cannot contain**? How are you going to contain and hold back a flood?"

Then he shared with me insights he had received from meditating on the scripture. When a flood comes, it overflows everything. There is no way to contain a flood. If it could be contained, it would not be a flood.

When I read this scripture with this thought in mind, I knew he was right from a New Testament point of view.

Then as I looked into it in the light of the Old Testament, I came to the conclusion that the King James Bible punctuation was right for those under the old covenant. For if they did not keep the law, the enemy did come as a flood, and there was no power under the law to stop him. It was as Solomon said. There was power on the side of the oppressor, but none for the oppressed. So for the people under the old covenant, there was no way of containing the enemy, once they stepped outside of the covenant.

The Tide Has Changed.

When we who are under the new covenant read this scripture, we are looking at it from a point of double reference. For in their day, they were facing the flood of the enemy without the power to contain him. So **they were looking forward to the Lord lifting up a standard against him.**

But today **we are living in the fulfillment of this scripture.** The standard has been lifted up. His arm (Jesus) brought salvation. The tide has turned, so to speak. **The Comforter has come. God has a man to stand in the gap** and make up the hedge. The Holy Ghost is in us, and the enemy can no longer come as a flood. **He can be contained.** Every fiery dart can be quenched. Today the flood is coming from the believers, and Satan can't stop it. Just as God did for Job, so has He turned our captivity, and now the flood has Satan captive today. **It is the flood of God's Spirit.**

So let's re-punctuate verse 19 and look at it from the vantage point of the new covenant.

When the enemy shall come in, *like a flood the Spirit of the Lord shall lift up a standard against him.* (Isaiah 59:19)

Flood Of God's Word And Spirit Puts Enemy To Flight.

I want to point out something about the word "lift." The center column reference in my Bible says, *or, "put him to flight."* So let's read it this way. *When the enemy shall come in,* **like a flood the Spirit of the Lord shall put him to flight.**

I believe this is proof enough that the punctuation is wrong in this particular verse, especially in the light of the new covenant. If the enemy is uncontainable, then you cannot put him to flight. How are you going to restrain him? It would be impossible for the enemy to come in as a flood, and also be put to flight.

There is no way to contain or restrain a flood. But thank God, under the new covenant, Satan can be contained and restrained.

71

To see this from a New Testament point of view, the main point of verse 19 is saying, **Like a flood the Spirit of the Lord will lift up a standard against him and he will have to flee.**

The word "flood" means rivers of water, a flowing stream, especially the Nile river. In other words, it was a flowing, rushing stream; something that's moving and overflowing banks. The Nile overflowed in the rainy season, and it was not containable.

But under the new covenant, when the enemy comes in, then like a flood the Spirit of the Lord will lift up a standard and put him to flight.

The devil would like to keep this scripture reversed in your thinking so you would believe it's the enemy who is coming like a flood today. But today it's the flood of the Spirit of the Lord that puts him to flight.

Now keep this thought in mind as we go to John, chapter seven.

> *37 In the last day, that great day of the feast, Jesus stood and cried, saying, If any man thirst, let him come unto me and drink.*
>
> *38 He that believeth on me, as the scripture hath said, out of his belly shall flow rivers of living water.*
>
> *39 (But this spake he of the Spirit, which they that believe on him should receive: for the Holy Ghost was not yet given; because that Jesus was not yet glorified.) (John 7:37-39)*

Remember, the word "flood" means flowing streams. That flood will come out of you. After the fulfillment of this scripture, the flood is referring to the flood of the Holy Spirit coming out of your innermost being—your spirit. The Bible calls it the belly.

Today the Holy Spirit abides in the believer's spirit. But under the old covenant, some things happened that couldn't be stopped, because the people did not have the Holy Spirit. The average layman in that day did not have communication with the Spirit of God. But Isaiah prophesied to our day that the enemy would be put to flight.

Let's look at verse 38 again.

38 He that believeth on me, as the scripture hath said, out of his belly shall flow rivers of living water. (John 7:38)

The word translated "belly" is an interesting word to study. It is used in the Old Testament as well as the New Testament.

Proverbs says,

The spirit of man is the candle of the Lord, searching all the inward parts of the belly. (Proverbs 20:27)

The belly refers to the center or core of man's being, or what we call the human spirit. Jesus was really saying, *out of your spirit.* The human spirit shall flow this flood that shall put the enemy to flight.

Our Weapons Are Not Carnal.

The apostle Paul gives us some light on this in Romans eight, when he says,

Likewise the Spirit also helpeth our infirmities: for we know not what we should pray for as we ought: but the Spirit itself maketh intercession for us with groanings which cannot be uttered. (Romans 8:26)

In other words, when the enemy comes in and we don't know how to pray, that river, that flowing stream of God's Spirit within us begins to release the flood.

When you don't know how to pray, pray out of your spirit in other tongues. I've been to the place physically and financially of not knowing how to pray. But I made it through by praying in the Spirit. When the enemy came in, the Holy Spirit began to pray through my Spirit. Out of my belly (spirit) came rivers of living water. That was the flood. It was the Spirit of God lifting up a standard against the enemy. And the enemy was contained.

Jesus Our Intercessor.

This is the flood for our day that was prophesied in Isaiah, chapter fifty-nine. The flood for those under the new covenant is not the devil and all of his problems. The flood is coming out of the believers' spirit. It is the Holy Spirit, flowing through their spirit, that is uncontainable. And Satan can't stop it. Out of their belly flows rivers of living water. That living water can flow out of you and nullify, cast down, and bring to nought all that the enemy has done. The Holy Spirit is the Comforter. He is the One called alongside to help. **Jesus is our intercessor.** He is seated at the righthand of the Father, making intercession for us. Jesus intercedes through your spirit, by the Holy Spirit.

Remember what Jesus said. "I'll not leave you comfortless. I will come unto you." Jesus came as the Spirit of truth. Jesus said the world couldn't receive Him. He said of the Comforter, *He dwelleth with you, and shall be in you.* (John 14:17)

Paul said the Holy Spirit, by your spirit, maketh interces-sion for us with groanings which cannot be uttered. The Greek says "can not be uttered in articulate speech, or in a language that you know." So when you don't know how to pray, pray in the Spirit, in other tongues. When you are in a situation where your back is to the wall, so to speak, pray in the Spirit. When you don't know what to do, pray in the Spirit, in other tongues. It is Jesus interceding through you.

God's Armor Is Ours.

13 Wherefore take unto you the whole armour of God, that ye may be able to withstand in the evil day, and having done all to stand.

14 Stand therefore, having your loins girt about with truth, and having on the breastplate of righteousness;

15 And your feet shod with the preparation of the gospel of peace;

16 Above all, taking the shield of faith, wherewith ye shall be able to quench all the fiery darts of the wicked. (Ephesians 13-16)

By taking the shield of faith **you** shall be able to quench all the fiery darts. **You shall be able to quench them. All of them.**

Now remember, a flood cannot be contained. Paul is tell-ing you that the enemy's attack can be contained. You can quench the fiery darts of the wicked one. You can quench anything the devil brings against you.

Let's read verses 17-18 together as one statement, and punctuate it differently. Allow me to share from this angle. Then you decide.

*And take the helmet of salvation, and the sword of the spirit, which is the **word of God praying always with all prayer and supplication in the Spirit**. . . .* (Ephesians 6:17-18)

In other words, the sword of the Spirit is the Word of God praying.

Let me say it another way. It is the Holy Spirit, through your spirit, praying the Word of God.

Jesus is our intercessor. Jesus is now equal with God, and He is seated at the right hand of the Father. He is glorified. He is back in His Godhead powers.

Then if Jesus were to pray, He would pray like God would pray, and **He is** making intercession for us.

But is it legal for Jesus to pray for us, now that He is in heaven and equal with God?

Jesus In You.

Now follow carefully what I am saying, for I am not going into this fully, but I do want to share with you some food for thought.

I'm not so sure that it would be legal for God to pray for us from heaven. According to Genesis one, God gave man dominion over the earth, and told him to subdue it. But Jesus came inside you when you were born again. He said to the disciples, "He dwelleth with you, but shall be in you." We know Jesus intercedes for us. I believe He does it through **your** Spirit, and through **your** voice. I believe it is the Spirit of truth, through your spirit, praying the Word of God.

If God were to pray for you, He would pray His Word over you. **God wouldn't say one thing in prayer that**

He hasn't already said in His Word. If you had lack, He would pray abundance over you. If you were in darkness, He would pray light over you.

Jesus is our intercessor, and He speaks only what He hears His Father say. So Jesus our intercessor would be praying the Word of God over us.

In Ephesians 6:17-18, Paul infers that the sword of the Spirit is the Word of God praying. He is not referring to the sword of the Holy Spirit, but rather, the sword of the human spirit.

We have said the Word of God is the sword. But the Word of God is not a sword until it's in your mouth. God's Word spoken out of your mouth becomes the sword of your human spirit. So the sword of the human spirit is the Word of God being prayed through your spirit.

When you pray in the Spirit you are praying God's Word over the situation.

> *27 And he that searcheth the hearts knoweth what is the mind of the Spirit, because he maketh intercession for the saints according to the will of God.*
>
> *28 And we know that all things work together for good to them that love God, to them who are the called according to his purpose.* (Romans 8:27-28)

When you pray in the Spirit, then you know that "all things" you prayed will work together for good, because you prayed the way God would pray.

Flood Of God's Spirit.

Under the new covenant, the enemy can be contained.

77

Believers are the ones who have the flood. The flood is the Holy Spirit, flowing out of our spirit. When the enemy comes in, then like a flood, the Spirit of the Lord will raise up the standard.

What is the standard? God's Word is the standard He is going to raise up against the devil. He will stop the devil with the Word of God.

I shared all of that to give insight into some reasons why many things happened under the old covenant, but should never happen under the new covenant.

God Provided Better Things For Us.

Return to Hebrews, to our foundation scriptures in chapter eleven.

37 They were stoned, they were sawn asunder, were tempted, were slain with the sword: they wandered about in sheepskins and goatskins; being destitute, afflicted, tormented;

38 (Of whom the world was not worthy:) they wandered in deserts, and in mountains, and in dens and caves of the earth.

39 And these all, having obtained a good report through faith, received not the promise:

40 God having provided some better thing for us, that they without us should not be made perfect. (Hebrews 11:37-40)

The "promise" of verse 39 refers to the promised Messiah. They didn't see the fulfillment of that promise in their day.

Notice this phrase, ***God having provided some better thing for us. . . .*** (v.40) There are people who want to identify with the others of Hebrews eleven. Let's identify with verse 40 which says that God has provided some better thing for us. We are not obligated to all the things they suffered under the old covenant. We have a better covenant. It is established on better promises.

Some Went Beyond The Call Of Duty.

If it were necessary for the gospel's sake, we should be willing to suffer. There are some places in the world today where they do suffer for preaching the gospel.

I am convinced that under this new covenant God has made a way of escape from every problem the enemy brings. Some didn't find it, and others didn't take the way of escape, even though they found it.

Paul kept going to the Jews, even when he was sent to the Gentiles. And nearly every time he preached to the Jews, he was stoned or thrown in jail. Paul went beyond the call of duty.

God Made Way of Escape.

On one occasion Paul was let down a wall in a basket. They surrounded the city of Damascus with a garrison to catch Paul, and they let him down the wall in a basket, and he escaped. God made a way of escape for Paul, and he took it.

Yet, in Acts twenty-one, Paul did not choose the way of escape, even though the prophet Agabus revealed what the Holy Ghost said would happen to Paul if he went to Jerusalem.

10 And as we tarried there many days, there came down from Judaea a certain prophet, named Agabus.

11 And when he was come unto us, he took Paul's girdle, and bound his own hands and feet, and said, Thus saith the Holy Ghost, So shall the Jews at Jerusalem bind the man that owneth this girdle, and shall deliver him into the hands of the Gentiles. (Acts 21:10-11)

He was telling Paul what the Holy Ghost was saying about him going to Jerusalem. This warning came by supernatural revelation of the Holy Ghost. But Paul said, "That doesn't move me. I'm going anyway."

God made known to Paul a way of escape. He sent a prophet of God to say, "Paul, if you go to Jerusalem, you're going to be bound."

Paul thought that it was just men who were going to bind him. But first of all, Paul allowed religious tradition to bind him in Jerusalem. He went there and compromised the Word. He even made a vow and did some religious things that were not under the new covenant, just to please the Jews. He got in a heap of trouble, and the end result was that he was bound, just as the Holy Ghost revealed by Agabus the prophet.

Did Paul miss God?

It appears that he did. But I'll not be the judge. Let's say he went beyond the call of duty. God made a way of escape. But Paul chose not to take it.

Some Did Not Choose Escape.

This explains many of the things that happened under the old covenant, and even some under the new covenant. Some had a way of escape, but they didn't choose to take it.

Paul did take the way of escape at Damascus, and he was

let down the wall in a basket. But on the other hand, he heard the prophet Agabus reveal to him, "If you go to Jerusalem, you will be bound."

To that, Paul replied, "That doesn't move me. I am going anyway."

Maybe Paul said, "This is too important. So I'm going anyway."

So we can't blame God for what happened. Paul chose to go beyond the call of duty.

It is a mistake for us to try to identify with the others of Hebrews eleven, because we have a better covenant. We have an intercessor. Let's identify with those who subdued kingdoms and wrought righteousness.

Underlined Scriptures Locate you.

You can look at the scriptures underlined in someone's Bible, and you can tell what they are believing. Those scriptures will locate them. If they are having pity parties, if they think they are another Job, if they think they're the "others" of Hebrews eleven, they will have underlined the scriptures on suffering.

But a person who has faith in the Word of God and the power of God to deliver from every situation will have the faith scriptures underlined. They will have marked those who through faith subdued kingdoms, wrought righteousness, escaped the edge of the sword.

If You Think Wrong, You Believe Wrong.

That tells you a great deal about the individual and how

they are thinking. For when you think wrong, you believe wrong. Then when you believe wrong, you act wrong.

I believe one of the most common mistakes made today is that of people trying to relate their life to the things that happened under the old covenant.

We have a new covenant, a better covenant. It is established on better promises. Hebrews 11:40 says, *God having provided some better thing for us. . . .* He has provided **a better covenant** for us. The old covenant was not as good as the new covenant and God found fault with it.

We should not expect to have the same problems they had under that covenant. God saw that it was not perfect, and He changed it. He provided something better for us.

More Promises Produces More Faith.

Some will say, "Do you think that you have more faith than the people of the old covenant?"

Well, let's think about that for just a minute. **Why wouldn't we have more faith** than the people under the old covenant, when the old covenant did not contain the promises that we have under the new covenant? No place in the Old Testament says, "Resist the devil and he will flee from you." Not one place under the old covenant says, "In Jesus' Name cast out demons."

Under the old covenant there was no power on the side of those who were oppressed. The only ability they had to escape those things was to stay under that covenant of promise, which was their umbrella of protection. When they did, then they were under God's protection. But if they did not keep that covenant, they were under the curse.

Redeemed From The Curse.

There is good news in the new covenant. Galatians 3:13-14 tells us, *Christ has redeemed us from the curse of the law, being made a curse for us . . . That the blessing of Abraham might come on the Gentiles through Jesus Christ.*

Every believer is considered to be of the seed of Abraham. He didn't redeem us from the blessing, He redeemed us from the curse. Abraham's blessings are ours under the new covenant.

Heirs Of The Promise Through Faith.

And if ye be Christ's, then are ye Abraham's seed, and heirs according to the promise. (Galatians 3:29)

What promise is he referring to here? The promise God made to Abraham. Romans, chapter four, records that promise.

For the promise, that he should be the heir of the world was not to Abraham, or to his seed, through the law, but through the righteousness of faith. (Romans 4:13)

Also in Romans, Paul said **the righteousness which is of faith** says,

The word is nigh thee, even in thy mouth, and in thy heart: that is, the word of faith, which we preach. (Romans 10:8)

Submit yourselves therefore to God. Resist the devil, and he will flee from you. (James 4:7)

83

Every believer should have more faith under the new covenant than any of the people under the old covenant. The new covenant is established upon better promises. You couldn't have faith to believe God for deliverance if there was not a promise of deliverance. But we have the promises.

We are **redeemed** from the curse of the law. So don't try to identify with the things that happened under the old covenant. For we are under a new and better covenant. Many of the Old Testament saints suffered so we could have the gospel. So let's walk in the light of what we have today.

Remember, Paul said, *Faith cometh by hearing, and hearing by the word of God.* So if you hear God's Word of promise, you can have faith for it.

The Old Testament saints didn't have the Word of promise that we have. They saw them afar off. But today, the Word is nigh you, even in your mouth, and then in your heart. So we should have more faith. For we have more and better promises.

Chapter 5

THE TRYING OF YOUR FAITH

22 Flee also youthful lusts: but follow righteousness, faith, charity, peace, with them that call on the Lord out of a pure heart.

23 But foolish and unlearned questions avoid, knowing that they do gender strifes. (2nd Timothy 2:22-23)

You can't always avoid foolish and unlearned questions. Some of the things we are sharing in this book will come up from time to time. Some of the questions you will be asked regarding these scriptures will seem to be foolish questions. To you, it may seem foolish, when you have insight into it. But then, no question is foolish, if you don't know the answer.

24 And the servant of the Lord must not strive; but be gentle unto all men, apt to teach, patient,

25 In meekness instructing those that oppose themselves if God peradventure will give them repentance to the acknowledging of the truth. (2nd Timothy 2:24-25)

Don't Lose While Winning.

I've said this several times in different ways, but I want to say it again. You have to teach people so that they will be willing to acknowledge the truth. You can win an argument sometimes, and prove your point. But if you are too dogmatic about it, you may lose the individual. They may not receive what you have to say. You may be right, and you may be able to prove from the scriptures that you're right. But the Bible says, . . . *the sweetness of the lips increaseth learning.* (Proverbs 16:21)

So if you have won the argument in such a way that the individual will not receive the truth, then you have failed.

In meekness we are to instruct those who oppose themselves. While teaching or preaching, we shouldn't present ourselves as being high and mighty. We mustn't have the attitude, "I just know so much more than you, and I am putting you down and showing you where you are wrong."

Sure, many people are wrong, and their ideas don't agree with God's Word. But you have also been wrong about some things

We must use wisdom to reveal the truth.

Paul goes on to say,

26 And that they may recover themselves out of the snare of the devil, who are taken captive by him at his will. (2nd Timothy 2:26)

In other words, the devil has taken them captive. Perhaps you were taken captive the same way by religious ideas and religious thinking about certain scriptures in the Bible. Those ideas held you in bondage until you learned the truth.

Food For The Spirit.

We entitled this book, "Kicking Over Sacred Cows." Sacred cows are worshipped in India. Some wouldn't dare eat them. But they worship them.

Some people worship the Bible. They wouldn't dare believe or act on what it said. They just worship it.

To so many Christians, the trials, troubles, and problems of life have become sacred cows. They believe that these problems perfect them. But here is what James said about it.

1 James, a servant of God and of the Lord Jesus Christ, to the twelve tribes which are scattered abroad, greeting.

2 My brethren, count it all joy when ye fall into diver temptations:

3 Knowing this, that the trying of your faith worketh patience.

4 But let patience have her perfect work, that ye may be perfect and entire, wanting nothing. (James 1:1-4)

Notice he didn't say, "the trying of your faith makes it stronger." But that's what most people believe—when your faith is tried, it becomes stronger.

You may come out of a trial stronger. But if you do, it is because you acted on the Word of God. It is not a direct result of the trial. The trial just gave you an opportunity to put God's Word to work in your life.

The Joy Of Knowing.

You are to *count it all joy when you fall into different temptations.* He didn't say, Count it all joy when you jump into temptation. That's what some have done. They didn't fall into it. They knew it was there, and they jumped into it.

Jesus said to pray that you not be led into temptation. We are to avoid these situations. But if you fall into a temptation, test, or trial, count it joy, *knowing this, that the trying of your faith worketh patience.*

But if you don't know that the trying of your faith calls for the force of patience, then you will be upset about the pressures of life.

Calling Patience To Work.

To be able to count it joy, you **have to know that the trying of your faith will call for patience.** Patience is a spiritual force. It is needed most when you are in a trial or a test of your faith.

To be patient means to be constant through the trial. You started out believing, "My God has met my need according to His riches in glory by Christ Jesus." (Philippians 4:19) You have the promise of Philippians 4:19, and you have set your goal **"My God has met my need."**

Patience Is A Perfect Work.

About a week later, it looks like all hell broke loose; you lost your job, the car broke down, and the kids came down sick. Then your faith begins to sag like a long bridge without pier under it. This is where patience comes in, to have its perfect work.

James didn't say the trying of your faith perfects it. He said the trying of your faith puts patience to work.

If you are patient, this force of patience will be like a pier under the bridge. It will hold up your faith when there is a long span of time from the time you believed you received until the time you actually receive.

Patience reinforces and undergirds your faith like a pier under a bridge. It helps you to remain constant in what you believe. Patience, allowed to do its perfect work, will support your faith until it quenches all that the enemy brings. Through faith and patience you receive the promise. You can count it all joy when you fall into temptation, if you know the outcome.

The Will Of The Kingdom.

In Matthew six, Jesus said something which will add some light to this. He was teaching His disciples to pray.

9 After this manner therefore pray ye: Our Father which art in heaven, Hallowed be thy name.

10 Thy kingdom come, Thy will be done in earth, as it is in heaven. (Matthew 6:9-10)

Jesus told the disciples to pray that the kingdom of God

would come, and that the will of God be done on earth, as it is in heaven. This must be the will of God.

There are some who ask, "Isn't it God's will for us to be in trials and tests? Isn't it the tests and trials that make us grow and become more like Jesus?"

The answer is no.

The tests and trials come to take God's Word out of you. They were designed to make you fail, and go back into sin. Mark the fourth chapter, brings this out.

Jesus said Satan comes to steal the Word. Jesus names five ways Satan steals the word of promise—afflictions, persecutions, cares of this world, deceitfulness of riches, and lusts of other things.

The word "afflictions" means pressures of life. It is these pressures of life that get to most people. You don't usually find people giving up when they are winning victories and things are going well. But it's when they are in troubles, trials, and tests that they usually foul out in the game of life and finally quit.

Remember, Jesus said for the disciples to pray that the will of God be done in earth, as it is in heaven. If Jesus said for the disciples to pray that way, then that has to be the will of God for the earth. Certainly, Jesus wouldn't tell His disciples to pray something that was out of the will of God.

Matthew 6:10 is one of the most profound scriptures in the Bible concerning God's will for the earth. *. . . thy will be done in earth, as it is in heaven.*

Deliver Us From Evil.

Then from verse 13 came another astounding truth.

And lead us not into temptation, but deliver us from evil: For thine is the kingdom, and the power, and the glory, forever. Amen. (Matthew 6:13)

Jesus said, pray that you won't be led in any way that you be tempted, tested, or tried, and deliver us from evil.

Right in the middle of this verse He says, . . . *deliver us from evil.* Why would he be talking about temptation, and all of a sudden say, *deliver us from evil?*

Jesus is calling the temptation "evil." This word "temptation" is from the Greek word that is also translated "trial and test." Jesus seems to say there is no good in it. It's not designed for any good.

It may be true that you will be stronger after a trial, temptation or trouble. But there was no power, no ability in that trial to make you more like Jesus. It was your decision to act on the Word of God that caused you to come out of it stronger.

Now follow this—if He said to pray that you not be led into temptation, then it's not God's will for you to be in temptation, test, or trial. God knows your weakness. God knows the situations in your life—where you are strong, and where you are not as strong.

Some people can hardly resist certain things. Then, those individuals ought to pray that God would lead them away from those things, and get them a job where they wouldn't be exposed to those particular things.

91

Heaven Is Free From Trials.

Now let's go back to this thought, *Thy kingdom come. Thy will be done in earth, as it is in heaven.* If it is the will of God for it to be done in earth, as it is in heaven, then ask yourself this: How is it in heaven? Are there any trials, any tests, any problems there?

We have learned from the scripture that there will not be any of these in heaven. Therefore, that tells us something about God's will for the earth. If God's will is for it to be on earth the same as it is in heaven, then the will for heaven is the will for the earth.

Let me say it in a different way. God's will for the earth is that it have what is already being experienced in heaven.

Then, if it were true that it is God's will for you to always be having trials or tests, and always be having problems here on earth, then you'd better get ready for trials when you get to heaven.

But we know that is not true, because we've read the back of the book and we found those things won't be in heaven. What Jesus said here is true, **the will of God for the earth is the same will as it is for heaven.** When you get to heaven you will not have any trials and tests and troubles and problems. **That is also the will of God for the earth now.**

Someone said, "Well, why in the world are we having so many problems, if it's not God's will?"

There are many reasons why we are having troubles and problems . . . **Mostly, it's because of sin and wicked men.** Then also, it's because **we don't always obey God.**

We don't always act on the Word of God, and we don't always act as God would act in every situation.

The Kingdom Within You.

When Jesus referred to the kingdom in Matthew 6:10, He was talking about the kingdom that would come to the earth on the day of Pentecost. The kingdom that is in the believers today.

In Luke 17:21 Jesus said, *. . . behold, the kingdom of God is within you.* Jesus seemed to say that when the kingdom comes, **then it will be possible** that the will of God can be done on earth, as it is in heaven.

You have the power and the ability through Christ and by the authority of the name of Jesus to cause things to change here on earth. You have authority to use the name of Jesus. **If you resist the devil, he will flee from you. We have power under the new covenant that people did not have under the old covenant.** We have the Spirit of truth within us.

God Moves His Throne To Earth.

As we read Revelation, chapter twenty-one, we get some insight into the changes that are coming to the earth.

2 And I John saw the holy city, new Jerusalem, coming down from God out of heaven, prepared as a bride adorned for her husband.

3 And I heard a great voice out of heaven saying, Behold, the

tabernacle of God is with men, and he will dwell with them, and they shall be his people, and God himself shall be with them, and be their God.
4 And God shall wipe away all tears from their eyes; and there shall be no more death, neither sorrow, nor crying, neither shall there be any more pain: for the former things are passed away.
(Revelation 21:2-4)

In other words, God is moving heaven to earth.

God's Will For Earth Has Not Changed.

It is the will of God for it to be on earth, as it is in heaven. **It has always been the will of God** that it be on earth, as it is in heaven. **It will always be the will of God** for it to be on earth, as it is in heaven. God intended for this earth to be a duplication of heaven itself.

But it took Adam only three chapters to mess it up. Things are still happening in the earth today because of the decision Adam made. He chose to eat of the tree of the knowledge of blessing and calamity, and it passed on to all men.

We must realize it is God's will for it to be on earth, as it is in heaven—for in the end it will be that way. God Himself will move here to make sure there is heaven on this planet. If it didn't turn out that way, we could say, "Well, maybe it wasn't God's will." But we know the end results. There will be a new earth, just as God has always desired.

Heaven is coming to earth. Righteousness will reign. This has always been the will of God. It is God's will for today, even though it has not yet come to pass.

Fiery Trials Are Not Strange.

Now let's look at another passage of scripture that is quite often misunderstood.

Beloved, think it not strange concerning the fiery trial which is to try you, as though some strange thing happened unto you. (1st Peter 4:12)

You shouldn't think it's strange that you are going through some fiery trials. For the devil is out to destroy you. He is out to steal the Word of God from you.

Peter didn't say it was God sending the trials. It's the devil sending the fiery trials.

In Mark four, Jesus mentioned five things Satan uses to steal the Word of God from you.

Affliction From Satan.

Satan's number one weapon is affliction. That doesn't just mean sickness and disease. But yet they would be included. The word translated "affliction" in Mark four means the pressures of life. That would include sickness, disease, financial problems, physical problems, and many others.

Satan's Only Hope.

All of these things are used by Satan to get the Word out to you.

What Word does Satan want out of you?

Specifically, it's the Word of Promise—that which God says in His Word belongs to you. Satan is out to get that

Word away from you. He knows, if he doesn't steal it from you, you will base your actions on that promise. His only hope is to stop you from acting on it by convincing you it will not work for you. You might hear God's Word and say, "Well, I wonder if that will really work? If I applied that in my business, would Mark 11:23 really work for me? If I were to say to this mountain of adversity, 'You will not hinder me. Be removed! Be cast into the sea!' If I believe and doubt not in my heart, would it really obey me?"

You might be pondering that course of action. Before you put it into action, Satan will try to stop you. That's his only hope. If you put the law of faith to work, he can't stop it from working. If you put God's principles into motion, eventually you will get the results God's Word promised.

But it takes time to develop faith in God's principles. Some think they can go to a faith seminar and come away a three-day wonder. But it takes time to develop your faith. You must practice those principles of faith.

Satan cannot steal the Word from you, if you understand it and become a doer of the Word.

The Enemy Steals What You Don't Understand.

Matthew's account says,

> When any one heareth the word of the kingdom, **and understandeth it not,** then cometh the wicked one, and catcheth away that which was sown in his heart. This is he which receive seed by the way side. (Matthew 13:19)

Your first step should be to get a good understanding

of the Word. Your first step should be to understand it and put it to work in your life. Then Satan can't steal it from you. Satan's only hope is to stop you from operating on God's principles. That's why Peter said, don't think it strange concerning the fiery trials, because that's what Satan is out to do—bring the fiery trials to stop you before you put it to work.

Arm Yourself With The Mind Of Christ.

First Peter 4:1 is what I would call a sacred cow scripture. So many people have allowed it to hold them in bondage.

Forasmuch then as Christ hath suffered for us in the flesh, arm yourselves likewise with the same mind: for he that hath suffered in the flesh hath ceased from sin. (1st Peter 4:1)

There are two sides to view in this scripture. It has double reference. We know it is referring to Jesus's death, because of chapter 3, verse 18.

For Christ also hath once suffered for sins, the just for the unjust, that he might bring us to God, being put to death in the flesh, but quickened by the Spirit. (1st Peter 3:18)

We must be careful in approaching verse 1 of chapter 4, lest we believe Peter is saying that we must be put to death as Jesus was put to death. Also, we must not get the idea that suffering is what makes us righteous.

Yet, we must realize, after we have been born-again, we must put to death some old desires of the flesh. Suffering the loss of fleshly desires is in the context of this scripture. But we must not take this scripture to mean the suffering of sickness and disease, or physical pain.

Lets look at this verse in the Amplified version.

So, since Christ suffered in the flesh [for us, for you], arm yourselves with the same thought and purpose [patiently to suffer rather than fail to please God]. For whoever has suffered in the flesh [having the mind of Christ] has done with [intentional] sin — has stopped pleasing himself and the world and pleases God. (1st Peter 4:1, Amplified)

I have an Amplified Bible. I think it's a good Bible. But some people don't read the front of the Amplified Bible to find out what these square brackets mean.

If you read that scripture, not knowing these square brackets mean that this phrase, *[patiently to suffer rather than to fail to please God]*, was added by the translators, you would be misled. That is not in the text. That's what somebody thought this verse of Scripture said.

Don't Take Translators' Ideas As Gospel.

Learn how to use the Amplified Bible. Be sure to read all of the information in the front of it. It tells you why brackets and other symbols are there. You will understand that this is not gospel when they put it in brackets, but is their own idea.

Learn how to use other translations also.

Christ Suffered For Us.

Now let's look at this verse from a different angle. Even though this view may not be the specific context, yet by dual reference, this is a powerful scripture for healing. *Forasmuch then as Christ hath suffered for us. . . .* Notice,

Christ suffered for us. If He did suffer for me, then He did it **so I wouldn't have to suffer the same thing.**

Matthew 8:17 tells us that Jesus *took our infirmities, and bare our sicknesses.* Peter says, **Arm yourselves likewise with the same mind.**

What would be the same mind? The same mind would be that Jesus suffered it for me. Therefore, I don't have to suffer the same thing. Now remember, we are looking at this scripture from a point of dual reference. Sometimes, by approaching it from a different angle, we can understand it better.

Suppose you owed a note on your car, and you got a letter from a friend which said, "I paid your note for you, **so you be of the same mind.**" Would you read that letter and say, "My friend paid my note and wants me to be of the same mind, so I guess I'll have to pay it just like he did."?

No. You wouldn't think that way. **You would say, "If he paid it for me, that means I don't have to pay it."**

Christ **redeemed us** from the curse of the law. He bore our sickness and our diseases. **He bore them for us so we wouldn't have to bear them.**

Forasmuch then as Christ hath suffered for us in the flesh, **arm yourself with the same mind.** If someone suffered for you, that means they suffered it in your place so that you wouldn't have to pay it.

We can understand that principle in everything else in life. But when we come to great truths of the Bible, our religious thinking sometimes gets it twisted around, and we miss the whole point.

I believe the apostle Paul hit the nail on the head when he said, *the God of this world blinds the minds.* . . . (2nd Corinthians 4:4)

Armed With A Weapon.

Peter said, *Arm yourselves likewise with the same mind.* What does it mean to be "armed?"

If you say a man is armed, that means he has a weapon.

Peter is saying, "This information is a weapon, so arm yourself with this fact that Jesus suffered it for you."

Even though this may not be the specific context of first Peter four, this is a powerful scripture concerning healing, and concerning being delivered from the curse of the law, and having abundant life in Christ. But if you are not careful, religious tradition and man's ideas will make it of none effect, even to the point of holding you in bondage.

But if you look at it from this point of view, you will be "armed" with a weapon that is capable of defeating the devil. If Satan comes to you with sickness and disease, tell him that Jesus took your infirmities and bare your diseases.

Jesus Cured The Sin Problem.

For he that hath suffered in the flesh hath ceased from sin. The context of this is that of putting to death the wrong desires of the flesh. Yet I believe, because Jesus suffered for us, He has put away sin by the sacrifice of Himself.

In the New Testament, Jesus is referred to as the Word. In the Old Testament, Isaiah refers to Him as a Rod.

And there shall come forth a rod out of the stem of Jesse, and a Branch shall grow out of his roots. (Isaiah 11:1)

Aaron took his rod (which is a type of Jesus) and threw it down before Pharaoh, and it turned into a snake. Pharaoh had the magicians throw their rods down, and they became serpents also. But **the rod Aaron threw down turned into a king snake, and it swallowed up the other serpents.** (Exodus 7)

That's what Jesus did when He became sin for us— He swallowed up sin. He cured the sin problem. We don't have a sin problem today. But we do still have a sinner problem. Jesus cured the sin problem. First John 1:9 stops the sin problem.

If we confess our sins, he is faithful and just to forgive us our sins, and to cleanse us from all unrighteousness. (1st John 1:9)

Joseph Told God's Secrets.

There is a sacred cow in Genesis thirty-seven, where Joseph had a dream from God. God gave him a vision or a dream and showed him that he was going to be above his brethren, and that his brethren **were going to bow down before him.** Let's pick up the story in Genesis 37:5-10.

5 And Joseph dreamed a dream, and he told it his brethren: and they hated him yet the more.

6 And he said unto them, Hear, I pray you, this dream which I have dreamed:

7 For, behold, we were binding sheaves in the field, and lo, my sheaf arose, and also stood upright; and, behold, your sheaves stood round about, and made obeisance to my sheaf.

8 And his brethren said to him, Shalt thou indeed reign over us? or shalt thou indeed have dominion over us? And they hated him yet the more for his dreams, and for his words.

9 And he dreamed yet another dream, and told it his brethren, and said, Behold, I have dreamed a dream more; and, behold, the sun and moon and the eleven stars made obeisance to me.

10 And he told it to his father, and to his brethren: and his father rebuked him, and said unto him, What is this dream that thou hast dreamed? Shall I and thy mother and thy brethren indeed come to bow down ourselves to thee to the earth? (Genesis 37:5-10)

Joseph went out and told his brothers all that God showed him in the dream. He also told his father, and his father rebuked him in disbelief. Joseph told God's secret, and it almost got him killed.

Some say Joseph went through all these problems so God could get him into a place of authority in Egypt and cause that dream to come true.

But ask yourself this—don't you think God was able to bring the dream to pass without the help of the devil and evil men? God was the One Who gave him the dream, and He was fully able to bring it to pass without the help of the devil or wicked men.

Certainly God was able to do it, but Joseph told God's secret. The devil got in on the deal and tried to stop it. This should be a warning to us all, not to tell everything God reveals to us.

God may reveal to you personal things that are going to happen in your future, but He doesn't want you to let the devil in on it by telling everybody. You need to keep some things secret.

Satan tried to destroy Joseph, and almost succeeded. Joseph suffered many things because he told God's secret. Joseph didn't know any better. But all scripture is profitable for reproof, for rebuke, and for instruction. We can be instructed by this and know not to tell everything God reveals to us.

Not everything God reveals to you is a secret. But some things are secrets between you and God.

I am convinced, if Joseph hadn't told God's secret, he would have had favor and power in Egypt without all the trials, troubles, and time spent in prison.

God had a way of doing it. But when Joseph let the devil in on it, he suffered some things that were not necessary to God's plan. But God brought Joseph through to victory, because he wouldn't let go of the revelation God gave him.

Joseph Made The Best Of Every Situation.

Psalm 105:17-19 states that, . . . *the word of the Lord tried him.* The Word that God gave him tried him. In other words, the circumstances looked like it wasn't going to come to pass. But he kept believing what God showed him in that dream. **Joseph's attitude and faith put him above the circumstances,** regardless of where they put him. When Joseph was thrown in the well, he could have given in to self-pity. But he still had the dream in his heart. When they put him in prison, he eventually was the doer of everything in prison. **His attitude of making the best of every situation gave him favor.** Even though for a short time he had disfavor, he always ended up having favor in every situation.

This has been a sacred cow to many people. They believe it was God's will for Joseph to suffer all those trials and troubles, and that this was God's way of getting him in a position of power.

But I believe it was Satan using the pressures of life (afflictions) to try to steal the dream from him.

Let me admonish you to give some time and meditation to these things as you study. Don't just brush through them and say, "I heard brother So and So say this was the way it was, and I guess that's just the way it was, because he's a man of God." He probably is a man of God and doing the best he knows, but he may not give any time to meditating on the scriptures.

Read The Bible Like You Never Heard It Before.

Several years ago, the Lord said to me, "You need to forget every comment you have heard about the scripture and go back and read the Bible like you never heard it before."

That sounded strange to me. But I just simply did what the Lord said. I started reading the Bible like I had never heard if before. It became a different book to me. It changed my life.

Faith For Victory Through Fiery Trials.

Now let's go to another passage of scripture; Daniel three. This is the story of the three Hebrew children. Here is another sacred cow scripture that actually was put here to give us insight and faith for victory, but so many have allowed it to hold them in bondage.

Nebuchadnezzar had made the decree that anyone who didn't bow down and worship his image was going to be cast into the fiery furnace. We will pick up the story in the latter part of verse fifteen.

> *15 . . . but if ye worship not, ye shall be cast the same hour into the midst of a burning fiery furnace; and who is that God that shall deliver you out of my hands?*
>
> *16 Shadrach, Meshach, and Abednego, answered and said to the king, O Nebuchadnezzar, we are not careful to answer thee in this matter.*
>
> *17 If it be so, our God whom we serve is able to deliver us from the burning fiery furnace, and he will deliver us out of thine hand, O king.*
>
> *18 But if not, be it known unto thee, O king, that we will not serve thy gods, nor worship the golden image which thou hast set up.* (Daniel 3:15-18)

Almost all of the sermons I have ever heard preached from this scripture indicated that the three Hebrew children said, ***"If it be so that our God decides to deliver us, then He will. But if He decides not to deliver us, we won't serve your god."***

Now, that sounds good on the surface, until you look into it. Then it becomes totally ridiculous. Let me show you why.

First, let's look again at what Nebuchadnezzar said. *You will be thrown the same hour in the midst of a fiery furnace.*

Now follow this closely, or you will miss it.

105

Then they said, **If it be so . . .**

"If it be so" what?

If is be so **that you do what you said you were going to do and throw us into the furnace.**

God Will deliver Us.

Here is actually the essence of what they said.

If it be so that you do what you said you were going to do, and you do throw us in the furnace, then **our God, whom we serve, is able to deliver us out of the fiery furnace, and He will deliver us out of your hand, O king.**

I challenge you to study that out in the scripture. That is really what they were saying. They were not saying, "If our God decides to deliver us, He will, and if He doesn't decide to deliver us, we will burn."

Verse eighteen says, *But if not . . .* Let's examine this closely.

"If not . . ." what?

If you don't do what you said you were going to do. In other words, *If you change your mind, King, if you tell us now that you are not really going to throw us in the furnace, we still want you to know that we're not going to serve your god.* Lets take the phrase **But if not. . .** If this really meant, "If God doesn't deliver us," then this scripture makes no sense at all.

If our God does not deliver us, we will not serve thy gods, nor worship the golden image. It's very obvious, if God doesn't deliver them, they are not going to serve anybody's god, not even their God, for they would

106

be a cinder in about five minutes.

So that is the reason you can't interpret that scripture that way. They are not saying, "If our God decides to deliver us, He will; but if our God decides not to deliver us, we'll just burn for God "

No! They are saying, "Even if you decide not to throw us in the furnace, we will not serve your god. But if you do throw us in the furnace, our God will deliver us."

It is obvious that they are not going to serve anybody's god if they are burnt up.

They are making a decree. They are decreeing it by faith that their God will deliver.

Believe And Decree.

Thou shalt also decree a thing, and it shall be established unto thee: and the light shall shine upon thy ways. (Job 22:28)

They decreed something in faith. They said, "Our God, whom we serve, is not only able to deliver, but He will deliver us out of your hand."

In full gospel circles you don't find many people who doubt that God is able to deliver out of any situation. They will say, "Yes, I believe God is able."

But it's not a matter of just believing that God is **able.** You must believe that God is **willing to do it for you now.**

This is what the three Hebrew children believed. They made two decisions: "We are not going to serve your god," and, "Our God will deliver us out of your hand."

The king got so angry that he heated the furnace seven

times hotter. Then he called for the strongest men in his kingdom, and had these three thrown in the fiery furnace.

> . . . *and the furnace exceeding hot, the flame of the fire slew those men that took up Shadrach, Meshach, and Abednego.* (Daniel 3:22)

But it didn't change the three Hebrew children. They were steadfast. They were fully persuaded that God would deliver them. They did not let the traditions of man make the Word of God of no effect.

They Were Fully Persuaded.

The three Hebrew children not only believed that God was **able** to deliver them, but they also declared that **He would deliver them.**

There are so many who say, "You just never know what God will do." But you will know what He will do, if you believe His Word and become fully persuaded.

God's Word is given to you to set you free, not to hold you in bondage. **If you know** what God will do, He will always do it. He will do everything you believe Him to do. **He will do everything He said He would do.** Faith for God's provisions of protection comes by hearing God's Word of promise.

> *He sent his word, and healed them, and delivered them from their destruction.* (Psalms 107:20)

Chapter 6

YOKES-THOUGHTS-BURDENS

In this chapter we will continue dealing with certain scriptures that are what I call sacred cow scriptures, because they have actually held people in bondage. God sent His Word to us to set us free, and to cause us to be quickened according to the Word of God. But sometimes, because of preconceived ideas that people have, they miss God's provisions.

So many people think the trials and tests of life are ordained of God. But I want you to hear what Jesus said about this in Matthew eleven.

*Come unto me, all ye that labour and are heavy laden, and **I will give you rest.*** (Matthew 11:28)

The way some people talk and act, you would think this scripture reads, "Come unto Me, all ye that have no problems, and I will burden you down with all the problems and cares of life; then you will be able to suffer for Me."

Some people think we have to be burdened down in life in order to please God. But Jesus even told His disciples to pray that it be on earth, as it is in heaven. Here in Matthew 11:28, these words also come out of the mouth of Jesus: **Come unto me all ye that labour and are heavy laden,** (heavily burdened) **and I will give you rest.**

This is God's idea of good news. Sometimes, man's tradition takes the good news and turns it into bad news.

Custom-Made Yoke.

*Take **my yoke upon you,** and learn of me; for I am meek and lowly in heart: and ye shall find rest unto your souls.* (Matthew 11:29)

Most people today don't understand much about yokes. But in those days, people used a wooden yoke around an oxen's neck. It made their work easier, because it was hand made to fit the oxen. And if there was a knot in that yoke, it would rub that oxen raw in a certain place.

I can just imagine, when Jesus was saying this to His disciples, they were probably standing under an olive tree next to the workshop, watching a man work on a yoke that wasn't fitting properly.

Jesus, observing, said, "If you'll just come to Me, My yoke is custom made to fit you. Take My yoke upon you—for My yoke is easy, and My burden is light."

Burden Not From God.

People who are always burdened down with a heavy burden have not learned to take His yoke. Most of those people believe God gave them that burden. But Jesus said,

For my yoke is easy, and my burden is light. (Matthew 11:30)

So many people take on burdens that God never intended for them to have. That's the reason why many people get out of the ministry. They take upon themselves the burdens of other people, instead of casting them on the Lord.

Jesus said, *Take my yoke upon you . . . my yoke is easy, and my burden is light.*

While we are on that subject, look at what God had to say about burdens in Jeremiah twenty-three. Billy Rash and I taught in a seminar, and he preached on this. It was so good that I asked his permission to share it in this book.

33 And when this people, or the prophet, or a priest, shall ask thee, saying, What is the burden of the Lord? thou shalt then say unto them, What burden? I will even forsake you, saith the Lord.

34 And as for the prophet, and the priest, and the people, that shall say, The burden of the Lord, I will even punish that man and his house. (Jeremiah 23:33-34)

I know you have heard people say, "I have this heavy burden from the Lord." But Jesus said, *I will give you rest—My yoke is easy and My burden is light.*

Actually, the word "burden" means job task. It's not heavy load, as most people think of a burden. Then here

111

in Jeremiah, God says, "I'll punish you for saying *a burden from the Lord.*"

God is not laying heavy burdens on people. But the devil does. Sometimes we have joined up with the devil and said, "These heavy burdens are from the Lord."

Burden Of The Lord Mention No More.

And the burden of the Lord shall ye mention no more: for every man's word shall be his burden; for ye have perverted the words of the living God, of the Lord of hosts our God. (Jeremiah 23:36)

We need to get some things straight. I didn't say that. God said it. God wants to un-laden you of your heavy burdens. God wants to get the heavy load off you—not put it on you. **It's religion that burdens you down.** It's the problems and circumstances in life that burden you down.

God said no such thing. In fact, He said the opposite.

Ye Shall Not Say "Burden Of The Lord."

38 But since ye say, The burden of the Lord; therefore thus saith the Lord; Because ye say this word, The burden of the Lord, and I have sent unto you, saying, Ye shall not say, The burden of the Lord;

39 Therefore, behold, I, even I, will utterly forget you and I will forsake you, and the city that I gave you and your fathers, and cast you out of my presence. (Jeremiah 23:38-39)

I believe another sacred cow just tumbled over. We have had the wrong idea about burdens. This was meant to be good news, not bad news. But it's like Jesus said to the Pharisees in His day, "The traditions of men make the Word of God of no effect." (Mark 7:13)

I want you to know that God is on your side. God wants to help you. God is trying to un-laden you of your burden—not burden you down.

I think one of the major problems with some people, especially ministers, is that they take all of the burdens of the people upon themselves, and they can't handle it. Some of them get out of the ministry because of it. A few even end up in an institution. There are many ministers in institutions today because they took the burdens of all their congregation on themselves, instead of praying about them and releasing them to God.

Learn To Cast All Cares Upon Jesus.

God never intended for you to take the burdens of all the people on yourself. In fact, the New Testament admonishes us to cast all our cares upon Him. (1st Peter 5:7) You see, this is God's will and God's purpose.

Perhaps you are burdened down because you have been taking all of the cares and burdens of everyone who came to you with a prayer request. You prayed with them, but you took the care on yourself. **You didn't cast it over on the Lord.** If you had cast it over on the Lord, you wouldn't be burdened with it, but instead would thank God for the answer.

Now don't misunderstand me. You can intercede in the Spirit. But you need to cast the care of it on the Lord. You ministers, don't take all the cares of your congregation on yourself.

Sometimes people come to me and say, "Would you pray

for me about a certain situation?"

We would pray, and I thought we were in agreement. The Bible said, *If two of you shall agree, it shall be done. . . .* But when we are through praying, they say, "Just keep praying for me, Brother Capps. Keep praying for me."

No! I am not praying continually. I prayed in faith, and I'm through praying about it. When I released my faith, it's finished, as far as I'm concerned. I won't take that care on myself.

If you do take these cares on yourself, in a short time you won't be able to help anyone. You will have more burdens and problems than you know how to handle. That's why Jesus said, *Come unto Me . . . My yoke is easy, and My burden is light.* He said, "I'll teach you. Take My yoke. It is custom made. It won't rub you raw."

When you say "Amen", you ought to be through with it, if you prayed in faith, unless the Lord directs you to intercede in the Spirit.

God's Thoughts And Our Thoughts.

Now let's go to Isaiah fifty-five.

8 For my thoughts are not your thoughts, neither are your ways my ways, saith the Lord.

9 For as the heavens are higher than the earth, so are my ways higher than your ways, and my thoughts than your thoughts. (Isaiah 55:8-9)

These verses have become sacred cow scriptures to some people, who are then held in bondage by them. These verses were not designed to do so. But because of religious tradition and preconceived ideas, people have allowed this to hold them in bondage.

You hear people quote these verses and then say, "Yes, God's thoughts are higher than our thoughts. God's ways are higher than our ways."

That is what I call a false truth. I mean, **it is in the Bible.** The Bible does say that. But we must keep it in context, or it can be very misleading. It can be a false truth. For if God's ways **are** higher than our ways, and **we can't attain to God's ways,** that is bad news.

Now let's back up two verses and put it in context. Then you will have good news instead of bad news.

The Wicked Man's Thoughts.

6 Seek ye the Lord while he may be found, call ye upon him while he is near:

*7 **Let the wicked forsake his way, and the unrighteous man his thoughts: and let him return unto the Lord, and he will have mercy upon him; and to our God, for he will abundantly pardon.***

*8 **For my thoughts are not your thoughts, neither are your ways my ways, saith the Lord.*** (Isaiah 55:6-8)

When God says, *My thoughts are not your thoughts,* He is talking about the wicked man's thoughts. He is not talking about you, a born again, spirit filled believer. He's talking about wicked people who refuse the Word and will not repent.

Now you can understand how the devil takes good news and perverts it. These verses were written to set you free. But if they are quoted out of context, they actually become a sacred cow and hold you in bondage.

Truth Is Revealed In Context.

It takes time and meditation to understand the scriptures. Certainly, you can find all kinds of Bible scriptures that seem to say almost anything, if you take them out of context. But if you keep scriptures in their context, they will reveal truth.

Notice that Isaiah goes on to say,

10 For as the rain cometh down, and the snow from heaven and returneth not thither, but watereth the earth, and maketh it bring forth and bud, that it may give seed to the sower, and bread to the eater:

11 So shall my word be that goeth forth out of my mouth: it shall not return unto me void, but it shall accomplish that which I please, and it shall prosper in the thing whereto I sent it. (Isaiah 55:10-11)

God's Ways Can Be Our Ways.

In this chapter of Isaiah, God actually says the exact opposite of what most people thought He said. He is saying, "This Word I sent is like rain which comes down from heaven, and it causes the earth to bud, and causes it to bring forth fruit, and furnishes seed for the sower so that you can operate in My way. I've sent you the seed of My Word. Put it in your mouth and sow it. My ways will work for you, and you can operate in My ways."

That is good news. But men's religious ideas make the word unfruitful. Kick over those sacred cow ideas and hold fast to the truth, and the Word will produce for you. God's ways will work for you, if you work them.

God will teach you His ways. Jesus said,

Be ye therefore perfect, even as your Father which is in heaven is perfect. (Matthew 5:48)

Paul said,

Be ye therefore followers (imitators) *of God, as dear children.* (Ephesians 5:1)

To imitate God, we must operate in His ways. Yes, God's ways are higher than the ways of the wicked. But the righteous can walk in God's ways.

Do All Things Work Together For Good?

Let's look at Romans 8:28. This scripture has really been a source of confusion to some people. You hear it quoted for everything from car wrecks to suicide. It goes like this; "That was really bad about Brother So and So. But you know what the Bible says, *. . . all things work together for good."*

But the Bible really didn't mean that in the context in which they are using it. Yet, it is true that the apostle Paul said those words. But let's put it back in Bible context to finits true meaning.

25 But if we hope for that we see not, then do we with patience wait for it.

26 Likewise the Spirit also helpeth our infirmities: for we know not what we should pray for as we ought: but the Spirit itself maketh intercession for us with groanings which cannot be uttered. (Romans 8:25-26)

The Greek says, "cannot be uttered in articulate speech or in the language which you have learned."

Paul is saying the Holy Spirit will rise up within you when you don't know how to pray. He will pray with words which you could not utter in the language that you know.

What You Prayed About In The Spirit Works Together For Good.

27 And he that searcheth the hearts knoweth what is the mind of the Spirit, because he maketh intercession for the saints according to the will of God.

28 And we know that all things work together for good to them that love God, to them who are the called according to his purpose. (Romans 8:27-28)

We have all heard verse 28 quoted out of context. The apostle Paul is saying here, "When you pray in the Spirit, you allow the Holy Spirit to pray through your spirit in tongues, using a language that you don't know. You are praying according to the will of God. Then the things you prayed about in the Spirit will work together for good."

Back up to verse 27 and let me point this out to you.

*27 And he that searcheth the hearts knoweth what is the mind of the Spirit, because he maketh intercession for the saints **according to the will of God.*** (Romans 8:28)

If you check your King James Bible, you will notice that verse 27 contains a phrase, *according to the will of God.* The three words ***the will of*** are in italics, which means this phrase was not in the original text, but was added by the translator.

So, let's take it out and see what happens to this verse of scripture.

Praying According To God.

Here is what this verse actually said in the Greek.

> . . . *because he maketh intercession for the saints* **according to God.**

Instead of . . . *according to* **the will of God,** it says, **. . . *according to God.*** The meaning is this; "When you don't know how to pray about a situation, the Holy Spirit, through your spirit, will make intercession through your voice in other tongues by praying the way God would pray."

Praying The Word.

In Ephesians six, the apostle Paul tells us to take "the sword of the Spirit." (Ephesians 6:17)

God's Word is the sword of the human spirit, when it is in your mouth. Paul said, *taking the sword of the Spirit, which is the word of God: Praying always with all prayer.* (Ephesians 6:17b-18a)

I believe you are praying the Word of God when you pray in the Spirit. If God were to pray for you, He would pray the Word over you. Whatever He said in His Word is what He would pray.

Put God In Rememberance Of What He Said.

I believe, if we could get hold of this truth, it would solve

119

a lot of problems in life. You can go to God with the problems, or you can go to God with the answers to the problems. If you will **learn to pray the answers**, it will solve tremendous problems.

Pray the Word of God. God's Word is the answer. Remind God of what He said. His Word will accomplish that whereunto He sent it.

> *So shall my word be that goeth forth out of my mouth: it shall not return unto me void, but it* **shall accomplish that which I please, and it shall prosper in the thing whereto I sent it.** *(Isaiah 55:11)*

God said,

> *Put me in remembrance: let us plead together: declare thou that thou mayest be justified. (Isaiah 43:26)*

That doesn't mean God is forgetful. God is wanting you to speak it, so you will hear it. For faith cometh by hearing. He is wanting you to pray the Word of God. Pray the Word of God always with all prayer and supplication in the Spirit. (Ephesians 6:18) That's the way God would pray for you. He would pray the Word of God over you.

All Things Don't Work For Good.

So when Romans 8:27 says, *he maketh intercession for the saints according to God,* that is a powerful statement.

Then the context of verse 28 is this: after you have prayed according to God, **then** you know that all things you have prayed about will work together for good.

You see, the apostle Paul is the one who wrote this verse,

and he didn't even believe that everything which happened worked together for good. If it were true that all things did work together for good, then you would have to say, "Adam sinned, and it worked together for good; so I guess my sin will work together for good."

But you know that's a lie. That couldn't be true. It wasn't God's will for Adam to sin.

False Truth Equals Error.

It's not God's will for you to sin. Your sins are not going to work together for good. You see how people can take something that is true in its context, try to fit it in somewhere else where it doesn't belong, and make it a false truth. It even becomes error.

That's why I call Romans 8:28 a sacred cow scripture. So many Christians worship that scripture and quote it for every bad thing that happens. But **the apostle Paul didn't believe everything that happened over the whole earth worked for good.** He wrote to the church at Thessalonica and said,

> *Wherefore we should have come unto you, even I Paul, once and again; but Satan hindered us.* (1st Thessalonians 2:18)

The apostle Paul didn't even believe what he wrote, if it is taken out of context. Certainly he believed it in its setting, but not concerning everything. We make a mistake when we **try to** make Romans 8:28 fit into every situation in life, when Paul used it only in reference to praying in the Spirit.

Carrying Your Own Salvation Into Effect.

Philippians 2:12 is also a scripture that you've mostly heard quoted out of context. No doubt you have heard someone say, "Paul said to just work out your own salvation; and if you are really sincere about it, you will be all right."

But that's not true. You can be sincere, and be sincerely wrong. You could be sincere and miss God's plan altogether. Paul was not telling you to just work up your own plan of salvation. But that is the way so many people interpret it. Let's look at that verse in context.

12 Wherefore, my beloved, as ye have always obeyed, not as in my presence only, but now much more in my absence, work out your own salvation with fear and trembling,

13 For it is God which worketh in you both to will and to do of his good pleasure. (Philippians 2:12-13)

The concordant literal translation says, *Be carrying your own salvation into effect.*

That does put it in a different light. He's not telling you to work out your own plan of salvation. God has already given us His plan in Romans 10:9.

That if thou shalt confess with thy mouth the Lord Jesus and shalt believe in thine heart that God hath raised him from the dead, thou shalt be saved. (Romans 10:9)

Paul is telling us to carry it into effect. If you believe that Jesus is the Son of God, then put it into action. Have you ever confessed that Jesus is Lord, and have you made

Him Lord of your life? If you haven't, then you have not put God's plan into effect.

You may say, "Yes, I believe healing is in the atonement. I believe Jesus bore our sickness and our disease. I believe we are healed with His stripes."

Well, have you ever made that effective in your life? Have you ever set it in motion? Paul said, "Be carrying your salvation (deliverance) into effect."

You set God's Word in motion by acting on the Word concerning these promises. This is what Paul is referring to in verse 12. Don't allow this verse to hold you in bondage. Let it set you free.

Independent Of Circumstances.

Philippians 4:11 is another passage of scripture that has seemingly been a hinderance to many people.

10 But I rejoiced in the Lord greatly, that now at the last your care of me hath flourished again; wherein ye were also careful, but ye lacked opportunity.

11 Not that I speak in respect of want: **for I have learned, in whatsoever state I am, therewith to be content.** (Philippians 4:10-11)

This verse has been quoted over and over again by people who don't believe in prosperity. They say, "Well now, the apostle Paul says to just be content with whatever you have."

Paul is referring to the fact that their care for him had flourished again. In other words, they sent an offering to him again, and he said, "I don't speak to you concerning

123

a need, because I have learned, in whatsoever state I am, therewith to be content.''

One translation says, *I have learned, in whatsoever state I am, to be independent of circumstances.* In other words, Paul was saying, "I don't let circumstances dictate to me how I feel or how I act."

Paul was not saying, "I'm just going to be content with what I have, and I can't do anything about it." But that is the way so many have interpreted that scripture.

But this is a powerful statement by Paul: **I have learned, in whatever state I find myself, I will just be independent of circumstances.**

God wants you to operate independent of the circumstances of life.

Being Content.

Let's look at another scripture, in Hebrews thirteen.

Let your conversation be without covetousness; and be content with such things as ye have: for he hath said, I will never leave thee, nor forsake thee. (Hebrews 13:5)

There are people who interpret this to say you should not want anything beyond what you have. You should not try to use your faith to get things from God.

Let's read further and see if this is really true in the text.

6 So that we may boldly say, The Lord is my helper, and will not fear what man shall do unto me.

7 Remember them which have the rule over you, who have spoken unto you the word of God: whose faith follow, considering the end of their conversation.

8 Jesus Christ the same yesterday, and today, and for ever.

9 Be not carried about with divers and strange doctrines. For it is a good thing that the heart be established with grace; not with meats, which have not profited them that have been occupied therein. (Hebrews 13:6-9)

When you bring this into context, it makes quite a difference regarding what it says. Is this really saying we ought to be content with what we have, and not want anything else? Is this talking about finances? If so, why would Jesus say, *"Give and it shall be given unto you?"*

If we should be content with what we have, then we should not want to receive anything more. So we couldn't give, for if we give, Jesus said we would receive.

You can see, when you take a scripture out of context, you get in trouble right away.

The key to understanding verse 5 is found in verses 4 and 9.

4 Marriage is honourable in all, and the bed undefiled: but whoremongers and adulterers God will judge.

9 Be not carried about with divers and strange doctrines. For it is a good thing that the heart be established with grace; not with meats, which have not profited them that have been occupied therein. (Hebrews 13:4,9)

Verse 4 sets the stage for what is said in verse 5. In other words, don't covet someone else's wife.

Then verse 9 links the coveting with strange doctrine and meat not to be eaten. But you hear this **"be content"** scripture quoted more often in connection with finances—and that idea is not in this scripture.

125

Sacred Cows Produce Bondage—Truth Sets You Free.

5 Let your conversation (your way of life) be without covetousness.

If you keep this in context, it can't mean what some say it means. The apostle Paul says, *covet earnestly the best gifts*, referring to the gifts of the Spirit.

You will get into trouble every time you take truth out of context and try to make it **the** truth in every situation. It becomes a sacred cow, and it will hold you in bondage, even though it was designed to set you free. God gave you His Word to set you free. This is the gospel. **This is good news.** But if you take it out of context, it becomes bad news.

There are some things that the Bible says **we should covet.** *Covet earnestly the best gifts.*

If it were really true that we should always be content with such things as we have, this would be true. If a person has heard only about salvation, but had never heard about healing, they ought to be content just being saved and not healed.

But you know that idea is not in that scripture. If it were, you could carry it over into other things and say, if you haven't received the baptism in the Holy Spirit, then you ought to be content and not seek to be filled.

So we must be careful to keep these scriptures in context.

You Can Reign In Life.

There are some who oppose the faith message and the prosperity message. They seem to oppose the idea that we can walk in victory here on earth. But the apostle Paul said,

. . . they which receive abundance of grace and of the gift of righteousness shall reign in life by one, Jesus Christ. (Romans 5:17) The Amplified Bible says, *shall reign as kings in life through the One, Jesus Christ, the Messiah, the Anointed one.*

That's what the apostle Paul said about it. But people who have opposing ideas will underline the scripture that says to be content with such things as you have. They also underline the suffering scriptures. Those are the things they meditate on and study. Some will stay up all hours of the night trying to prove it's not God's will for them to enter in to the provision that God has provided for them.

Don't Be Ashamed Of The Gospel.

Paul said those who **receive the abundance** of grace and the gift of righteousness **would reign in life.** But some won't receive the abundance of grace. Would you rather be reigning in life, or burdened down under all the circumstances of life? You can put the circumstances under you by Jesus Christ. Receive the good news of the Word of God. The gospel is good news.

Don't be ashamed of the gospel, for it is the power of God unto salvation.

The good news is the power of God unto salvation, deliverance, preservation, and healing. The idea of prosperity is involved in the word "salvation." It is translated from a Greek word called "sozo." This is an all inclusive word which means preservation, healing, and soundness.

This is God's provision. But it is up to you to put it into effect.

Works Of God Brings Sight To The Blind.

Let's go to John nine, where we find another scripture that holds some people in bondage. It has become a hinderance to them, rather than a blessing, because they fail to rightly divide the Word.

1 And as Jesus passed by, he saw a man which was blind from his birth.

2 And his disciples asked him, saying, Master, who did sin, this man, or his parents, that he was born blind?

3 Jesus answered, Neither hath this man sinned, nor his parents: but that the works of God should be made manifest in him.

4 I must work the works of him that sent me, while it is day: the night cometh, when no man can work.

5 As long as I am in the world, I am the light of the world. (John 9:1-5)

When referring to this scripture, most people say, "Jesus said this man was born blind for the glory of God."

But **that is not what Jesus said** at all. Let me point out to you why you cannot interpret this scripture that way.

The question in verse 2 was really this: did the man's sin, or did his parents' sin cause him to be born blind? The disciples were looking for the answer in one of the two reasons they gave for the man's blindness.

Jesus could answer it three ways. It could be the man's sin, it could be the parents' sin, or He could say it was neither. Any one of those three answers would answer the question.

Jesus answered their question by saying neither of these reasons was right. They asked the question the way they did because the Jews believed that a child could sin in his mother's womb.

When Jesus said, *Neither hath this man sinned, nor his parents,* He didn't literally mean that none of them had ever sinned, for the Bible says all have sinned. Jesus is saying the man's sin was not the cause of the man's blindness, nor was the parents' sin the cause.

Jesus did not tell them why the man was born blind. He just simply stated that neither of these assumptions was right. Then Jesus makes this statement:

> 3 . . . but that the works of God should be made manifest in him. **I must work the works of him that sent me.** (John 9:3-4)

In other words, He said, "If the works of God are going to be manifest in this man, I will have to work them."

Common Sense Reveals Something.

Many people try to say that this blindness was the work of God, so that He could get glory out of it. But God is not causing people to be born blind and crippled so He can get glory out of healing them. **Common sense** would tell you that's not true. People who believe that way are held in bondage by their wrong thinking.

Look at it this way. If you could prove that someone here on earth was causing babies to be born blind or crippled, that person would be sent to the penitentiary. But yet, some people believe our Heavenly Father does those things.

Nothing could be further from the truth. That's the lie of the devil.

Jesus Works The Works Of God.

As you punctuate these verses correctly, it reads this way.

Neither has this man sinned nor his parents. A period should be placed after the word "parents." Then He makes the statement revealing what he must do.

But that the works of God should be made manifest in him, I must work the works of Him that sent me. . . .

Jesus is saying, *I am going to show you the works of God.* **It couldn't have been the work of God that caused the man to be born blind. For when Jesus worked the work of God in him, the man could see.**

Man's religious ideas cause this scripture to hold many in bondage. Some even underline these scriptures to try to prove that it's God's will for some to be born blind or crippled. They believe it is for some mysterious purpose, and somehow God gets glory from crippling some people for life.

But Jesus said it is the thief that comes to steal, to kill, and to destroy.

4 I must work the works of him that sent me, while it is day: the night cometh, when no man can work.

5 As long as I am in the world, I am the light of the world.

6 When he had thus spoken, he spat on the ground, and made clay of the spittle, and he anointed the eyes of the blind man with the clay.

7 And said unto him, Go, wash in the pool of Siloam, (which is by interpretation, sent.) He went his way therefore, and washed, and came seeing. (John 9:4-7)

Isn't it amazing, **when Jesus worked the work of**

God, the man wasn't blind any more. But some people will try to tell you that the blindness was from God. After Jesus worked the work of God and the man could see, it's very obvious that the blindness was the work of the devil.

It was not because of his parents' sin. It was not because of the man's sin. It was not because God wanted it that way. It was because of the enemy that comes to steal, to kill, to destroy.

Certain things happen sometimes because of deformed cells and genes. But the devil is behind it all.

Jesus Came To Destroy Works Of The Devil.

. . . for this purpose the Son of God was manifested, that he might destroy the works of the devil. (1st John 3:8)

That's what Jesus came to do—destroy the works of the devil. Here we find Him destroying the blindness. So the man's blindness had to be the work of the devil, not God. For Jesus said, *I must work the works of God.* God's work caused the blind man to be able to see.

Jesus Spoke End Results.

While we are on the subject of sacred cow scriptures, let's go to John eleven.

1 Now a certain man was sick, named Lazarus, of Bethany, the town of Mary and her sister Martha.

2 (It was that Mary which anointed the Lord with ointment, and wiped his feet with her hair, whose brother Lazarus was sick.)

131

3 Therefore his sisters sent unto him, saying, Lord, behold, he whom thou lovest is sick.

4 When Jesus heard that, he said, This sickness is not unto death, but for the glory of God, that the Son of God might be glorified thereby. (John 11:1-4)

Many people try to say that Jesus said Lazarus was sick "for the glory of God." But that idea is not in these verses. The rule of scriptural interpretation is to interpret scripture literally, if you can. But if you interpret the fourth verse literally, then it makes Jesus a liar. So we have to look at it from a different angle.

Jesus is actually saying, **the end results** of this whole matter will bring glory to God. **It was the resurrection that brought the glory,** not Lazarus' sickness, nor the death of Lazarus.

Some people say, "Well, if Lazarus was sick for the glory of God, then I'm probably sick for the glory of God."

So in some mysterious way, they believe God is getting glory out of their sickness.

But God doesn't get glory out of sickness. The devil gets the glory out of sickness.

In verse 4 Jesus established the fact that the end results of this matter will not be death, but will bring glory to God.

You can't interpret that verse literally, because Lazarus died. Jesus knew he was dead. But Jesus was declaring the end result. And the end result was the resurrection to life.

That was what brought glory to God. When in doubt of what is implied in certain scriptures, remember to always go back and meditate on John 10:10. This is the balance wheel of the Bible.

The thief cometh not, but for to steal, and to kill, and to destroy: ***I am come that they might have life, and that they might have it more abundantly.*** (John 10:10)

Charles Capps is a retired farmer, land developer and ordained minister who travels throughout the United States sharing the truth of God's Word. He has taught Bible seminars for over thirty years sharing how Christians can apply the Word to the circumstances of life and live victoriously.

In the mid 90's the Lord gave Charles an assignment to teach end-time events and a revelation of the coming of the Lord.

Besides authoring several books, including the best selling *The Tongue, A Creative Force*, and the mini book *God's Creative Power®*, which has sold over 4 million copies, Charles Capps Ministries has a national, daily syndicated radio and weekly television broadcast called "Concepts of Faith."

For a complete list of CDs, DVDs, and books
by Charles Capps, or to receive his publication,
Concepts of Faith, write:

Charles Capps Ministries
P.O. Box 69,
England, AR 72046

Or visit him on the Web at:
www.charlescapps.com

BOOKS BY CHARLES CAPPS

Triumph Over The Enemy

When Jesus Prays Through You

The Tongue – A Creative Force

Releasing the Ability of God Through Prayer

Your Spiritual Authority

Changing the Seen and Shaping The Unseen

Faith That Will Not Change

Faith and Confession

God's Creative Power® Will Work For You
(Also available in Spanish)

God's Creative Power® For Healing
(Also available in Spanish)

Success Motivation Through the Word

God's Image of You

Seedtime and Harvest
(Also available in Spanish)

Hope – A Partner To Faith
(Also available in Spanish)

How You Can Avoid Tragedy

Kicking Over Sacred Cows

The Substance of Things

The Light of Life in the Spirit of Man

Faith That Will Work For You

BOOKS BY CHARLES CAPPS
AND ANNETTE CAPPS

Angels

God's Creative Power® for Finances

God's Creative Power® – Gift Edition
(Also available in Spanish)

BOOKS BY ANNETTE CAPPS

Quantum Faith

Reverse The Curse in Your Body and Emotions

Understanding Persecution